# THE GREAT BOOK OF AMERICAN TRIVIA

## Fun Random Facts
## & American History

### TRIVIA USA VOL.2

## BY
## Bill O'Neill

ISBN-13: 978-1981454334

# DON'T FORGET YOUR FREE BOOKS

# CONTENTS

## CHAPTER SIX

## CHAPTER SEVEN

## CHAPTER EIGHT

# INTRODUCTION

The United States of America has a long and complex history—sometimes dark and sometimes colorful—full of tall tales, half-truths, and hard facts you'll find harder to believe than the myths. The history we learn as young children is the stuff of flowery fantasy in some cases, and it gets more honest and less interesting the older we get until we finish school. But we never get to the meat of it until we enter the real world and learn life isn't and never was that easy or perfect.

No one really knows for sure when the landmass now known as the United States of America first became inhabited by people, but like most of the rest of the world, it's not where humans originated, so all we can do is guess who they were and how long ago they came. Most well-educated guesses say the land became peopled when hunter-gatherers crossed Beringia from modern Russia into what we now know as Alaska, moving gradually south, likely in search of warmer climates.

The populations we refer to as Native Americans, or

1

indigenous peoples, may be their descendants, but in any case, they are the people who have longest resided on this land in modern history. They were the sole human residents of the landmass until Europeans arrived in the fifteenth century, and mostly from there is where the story begins, at least for this book. How the United States went from being unoccupied by humans to being one of the most populated countries in the world and the world's greatest superpower is a long, meandering, cacophonous story that might be better addressed in a complete set of encyclopedias rather than two-hundred-word vignettes that can only serve to peek behind the curtain.

This book of American trivia is meant to give a broad overview of the biggest events—admittedly with a few more trivial but very interesting tidbits along the way—in a way that delivers truth without getting into debate about bias. History can get dry, so humor is a great alleviator, but quite frankly, not all of it is very funny. Some of it is hard to hear, and some of it sparks debate, sometimes because of one's interpretation and sometimes because the version we learned hasn't been unlearned, and the new, not as pleasant information might come as a surprise.

This book won't change the world, and it isn't intended to, so hopefully any debates don't get too out of hand. I hope you learn something and you take it with you. It's intended to be as honest as possible, with pride in the United States but a healthy dose of reality in where we came from. Nothing's perfect, and some things are further from it than others, but truth is the only way to make sure one gets closer and closer to it. I hope you read this book with interest and sometimes maybe a little anger (though not at me), sometimes a lot of laughter, and you learn something about the United States, about your history, and about how even the things you love most in the world aren't perfect and really don't have to be, as long as you're willing to help get them a little closer.

---

# CHAPTER ONE

# NATIVE AMERICAN HISTORY

Let me be very clear in saying that Native American history is intertwined into the very fabric of US American history, so the topic doesn't really merit its own chapter but should instead be woven into and highlighted in every chapter in this trivia book. However, formats are sometimes limiting, and there is so much to say about just about every subject. The best way to make sure this bedrock history to the United States is properly included, and its significance made very, very clear instead of accidentally overlooked, is to dedicate a full chapter and put it right in the front. This is where the United States came from, no debate there.

That introduction feels necessary because this nation is historically viewed as being founded by European settlers, but there were already people on this land. The history of those indigenous people has been altered and systematically erased in many ways, but they're still here and a very strong, powerful, and important part of our culture, so the stories of their significance should not be mixed in with other European-based facts and possibly forgotten or minimized.

## Paleo-Indians

There is a lot of controversy over who the first inhabitants of North America were. Undoubtedly, the population we refer to as Native Americans were here before Europeans—Columbus himself is a documented witness—but where did they come from? Most evidence indicates they weren't native to the continent but came from Eurasia hunting animals over Beringia, the land and ice bridge that connected the two land masses as recently as 12,000 BC. The dates are still debated, but archaeologists believe the migration ended about 16,500 years ago.

They entered North America via modern Alaska, and made their way down the western coast and into the southern tip of modern South America. So, while indigenous North American communities were settled for thousands of years before the presence of modern America, the land mass wasn't originally inhabited by anyone.

## Hopewell

The Hopewell tradition wasn't a single culture, but a diverse and geographically spread out group of tribes connected along a river trade route in the Northeastern and Midwestern parts of the United States. Some sections extended as far as the southeastern United States up to Lake Ontario in southeastern Canada. The tradition was unique because it lasted for so long, from 200 BC to 500 AD.

They created some of the finest art pieces in the Americas, using natural materials from all over the trade route. Nothing was spared, using grizzly bear teeth, pearls, shells, copper, silver, and in at least one case, a human skull, to create exquisite jewelry. Hopewell was also known for the ceremonial mound building discussed next. Around 500 AD, the Hopewell exchange ceased, but no one is quite sure why. War is a possibility, as is relocation, but evidence remains vague.

## Conical mounds

Conical mounds are Native American constructions comparable to Egyptian pyramids, with symbolism and patterns that have been compared to the Nazca Lines of Peru. They are raised piles of earth that sometimes now just appear to be hills, built as effigies in the shapes of animals, humans, and other often spiritual symbols. They sometimes contain human remains but were used for religious purposes as well.

Dating back to 700 BC, the mounds are no longer constructed, but Native Americans still frequent them to visit and communicate with elders, give thanks, and put out offerings. Tribes in modern Wisconsin built more than any other area, and they became most widespread during the Hopewell period. Many have been lost to farming and development, but most known mounds are now federally protected from destruction.

## Mesa Verde cliff dwellings

Mesa Verde is in southwest Colorado and is now established as a national park to protect its architecture, in large part built into the sides of cliffs. The four thousand remaining structures, of which six hundred are cliffside, come from a community of Pueblo Anasazi Indians that was established as early as 400 AD. The most magnificent of the structures is the Cliff Palace, constructed of sandstone, wood, and mortar, and originally painted in brilliant colors.

The villages were abandoned around 1300 AD, and no one is sure why, but it may have been warfare, or it may have been drought. The area holds Mummy Lake, which archaeologists once believed was a reservoir but now believe was used for ceremony. Mesa Verde became a UNESCO World Heritage site in 1978.

## Taos Pueblo, New Mexico

This is a fascinating area in northern New Mexico where adobe structures have been inhabited without modernization for centuries. The Pueblo settlements date back to the thirteenth century along the Rio Grande, and Taos is one of several that have survived to present day. The Taos settlement is the largest still surviving and has resisted development, being the oldest continuously inhabited community in the country. It was originally part of the Spanish Land Grant and is now protected as a UNESCO World Heritage Site and National Historic Landmark. The community is known for being very private and secretive, and while it is a popular tourist destination, the approximate 150 full-time residents have closed off some areas and time periods to visitors.

## Native Americans and horses

Given that horses are not native to the United States and that they play a central role in Native American culture, the story of their introduction is rather interesting. The Spanish brought in horses, or at least modern horses. Actually, there *were* native horses, but they became extinct during the Paleo-Indian period, likely due to climate events or hunting. Escaped Spanish stallions and mares produced the wild horses that now roam mostly in western Plains areas of the nation. The horses were used for hunting and travel, increasing wealth but also warfare.

Indians first discovered horses while slaves to the Spanish, learning their value while training and riding them in their labor. In 1680, the Spanish were driven out of Pueblo areas so quickly they retreated without their horses, which the Pueblo Indians then used. They began selling and trading with other tribes, making them all better hunters and more nomadic.

## Iroquois Confederacy

This upper New York state-area group was also called the Six Nations, and were the Mohawk, Oneida, Onondaga, Cayuga, and Seneca, with the Tuscarora joining in 1722. They were a peacekeeping group to bring the tribes together and played a central role in the fight between the French and British for North America. The Confederacy was formed sometime around the dawn of the seventeenth century to protect the tribes against invasion. They weren't the only confederacy formed for this purpose in the volatile period, but they were the best organized and most effective by far.

They created the Great Law of Peace, an oral constitution thought to have inspired the United States Constitution. The

American Revolution was ultimately the fall of the Confederacy, with some tribes siding with the colonies and the rest loyalists. Now, the Onondaga, Seneca, and Tuscarora are mostly on reservations in New York, while Mohawk and Cayuga relocated to Canada. The Oneida wandered, some staying in New York and others moving into Wisconsin and Ontario.

## Mystery of Sacagawea's death

Sacagawea is known for helping Lewis and Clark explore the Louisiana Territory. She did a lot of interesting things, but probably the most fascinating thing about her life is actually the mystery surrounding her death. Historians report that she passed away on December 20, 1812, of typhus, leaving her children to be raised by Clark. But oral history of the Shoshone tradition says that she actually died in 1884, in Wyoming ancestral lands, where her eldest son and a younger son had lived with her. This story says that she left her husband after the expedition and died on the Wind River Indian Reservation on April 8, 1884.

This second story wasn't uncovered until 1924, when the Bureau of Indian Affairs sought to find her final resting place. In personal interviews with elders of her tribe, an investigator uncovered the oral histories of a woman who matched her description. The daughter she bore on the

Lewis and Clark expedition is believed to have died after 1812, as there are no stories of her life past infancy, but the second son from the Shoshone stories was born later.

## Trail of Tears

Between 1830 and 1850, Presidents Andrew Jackson and then Martin van Buren were responsible for the forced relocation of thousands of Native Americans from their ancestral homelands in the southeast to new territories in the west. The lands were desired for development, largely by farmers or for other natural resources. The removal was ordered for some slaves and black free men, but largely for the Five Civilized Tribes—Chickasaw, Choctaw, Creek, Seminole, and Cherokee—and the Trail of Tears moniker comes from the disastrous and heartbreaking Cherokee removal of 1838. This phase of the removal was particularly brutal, occurring in the winter through blizzard conditions with the displaced peoples wearing scant clothing and often without shoes, traveling on foot under the eyes and guns of militia.

While the Trail of Tears and other removals are a tragic part of the nation's history, what some don't realize is that they were illegal. The government cited the Indian Removal Act of 1830 as its authority for the journeys, but the act didn't permit relocation without an agreed-upon treaty. Rather, it authorized a mutually agreed-upon land exchange with the government paying moving costs. Instead, the Choctaw were moved in 1831, the Seminoles in 1832 after two bloody confrontations, the Creek in 1834, and the Chickasaw in 1837. While each removal was difficult and illegal, resulting in much loss of life, the Cherokee march was the most inhumane. Overall, about a quarter of Indians died on the marches.

## Indian Appropriations Act of 1871

After the 1851 act of the same name to move Indians onto reservations, the 1871 act stated that no new groups of Native Americans could be recognized as independent nations. Worse than this, Congress declared that all Native Americans were considered "wards" of the federal government. Prior to the act, the government had established several treaties with various tribes, guaranteeing land cessions from the Indians in exchange for annual payments and resources, but after the treaty, they declared these pacts null. As a result, the government seized lands without having to compensate.

Thus, the bill made it significantly easier for the government to usurp the properties in disregard for Native American rights and needs. It voided all previous treaties and forbade the making of new ones. Supposedly this shift came as result of a struggle between the House of Representatives and Senate over control of Indian affairs, and the power imbalance continued for a century until tribes were granted rights to operate as self-governing entities.

## Wounded Knee

Two days before the dawn of 1891, the US government attacked Lakota in Wounded Knee, South Dakota, in what was to be the last major battle of the Indian Wars. By then, forced removal was government policy, and that was the intent. While it wasn't the largest mass murder of Native Americans, with somewhere between one hundred and fifty and three hundred killed, it was important historically because it marked the symbolic end of Indian resistance to assimilation. Skirmishes continued after this event, but the government had officially lowered indigenous warriors' numbers enough that they could no longer resist effectively.

The incident occurred when governmental authorities arrived to "escort" the Lakota Sioux from their land. The forces were armed and surrounded the tribe. The Lakota also had weapons from previous interactions. The story says that one deaf Indian warrior did not heed orders to lay down weapons, and the chaos that ensued after his noncompliance led to the massacre. Popular history has painted the warrior to be a bad egg who possibly instigated the entire escalation, but Native American recollection does not support that version.

## Ishi

The Yahi are not permitted to tell their names unless they are introduced by another Yahi, but all members of the tribe excepting one were murdered in a genocide committed by settlers over a period of years. No one knew the survivor's name because there was no one to introduce him, so he adopted the name of "Ishi" which meant "man" in the Yana language.

Ishi, who was known as the last wild Indian, wasn't discovered until 1911, though the massacre that happened in 1866 destroyed his village, and there were some remaining members of his tribe attacked until at least 1871. In 1908, the three other Yahi he was living with—his mother, sister, and uncle—were subject to one final attack. His ailing mother was hidden while the other three fled. When Ishi returned, she died soon after, and the other two never returned and were presumed killed. He came out of hiding three years later, because he was starving living on his own, and was taken in at the University of California at Berkeley as a research assistant to an anthropologist. He died five years later of tuberculosis at the institution.

## Reservations in modern times

Indian reservations are lands managed by federally recognized tribes. There are more than three hundred reservations, with more than five hundred recognized tribes, so not all tribes have a reservation, while some have more than one and other reservations are shared. They were mostly established during forced removals as a designated area to move Native Americans to when being driven from their homes. Today, they are mostly self-governed, and about 22 percent of Native Americans live on them.

Some sociologists have compared living conditions on modern reservations to that of third world countries, due to housing shortages, unemployment, and other economic factors. Over 56 million acres of the United States are dedicated to the reservations, and despite self-governance, treaties, and agreements with the United States, they continue to have to battle for rights and recognition. Recent conflicts over land access in Standing Rock are good examples of this, and the stand-offs continue to this day.

## The history of Pine Ridge

Pine Ridge Reservation belongs to the Oglala Lakota Sioux, and it's the eighth largest in the world as well as the poorest. It holds other great significance in American history books as well. Custer's Last Stand happened near there, and Sitting Bull and Crazy Horse were famous Lakota chiefs. The Wounded Knee massacre happened there, and so did a 71-day stand-off in 1972.

There was a period of extended violence, and in 1975, two FBI agents and an Indian activist were killed in what is known as the Pine Ridge Shootout. The trial as a result of this event is what led to the imprisonment of Leonard Peltier, who is still serving two life sentences in what has proven to be a very contentious sentencing. Human rights workers and activists worldwide still fight for his release.

A modern view into the reservation finds that the trauma continues there. Statistics demonstrate 80 percent of the reservation is unemployed, and 98 percent live below the federal poverty level, with an infant mortality rate five times the national average, teen suicide quadruple the average, and life expectancy only climbing to the early 50s.

## Potlatch

A potlatch is a celebration of the indigenous of the Pacific Northwest, where a feast is thrown and gifts are exchanged. It is a social status competition of sorts where the gifts and destruction of property elevate or lower the status of respected members of the community, with members giving away their resources while receiving them in return.

For a period, it was banned by the government because the property destruction was deemed wasteful and un-Christian. The potlatches continued underground even though criminal punishments could be doled. Potlatches are also planned for events such as funerals, rites of passage, births, and marriages. They can take years to plan and last for weeks. Contrary to popular urban legend, the term "potluck" did not originate from "potlatch," though it makes a good story for two favorite American and Native American past-times.

# INTERESTING FACTS

1.  When Europeans arrived in the United States, there were eighteen to twenty million indigenous people. By the 2010 Census, there were only 5.2 million, just 1.1 percent of the total population. Forty-one percent of Native Americans live in the western part of the United States.

2.  Historically, the Cherokee are matrilineal. Being matrilineal means that the clanship of a child is decided based on which tribe the mother belongs to.

3.  Native Americans believed in using every part of the buffalo they killed. They could use the hide for clothing and housing, the meat for food, and even the horns for dishware.

4.  A variety of Indian words have made it into English language and everyday usage. These include the words skunk, bayou, hickory, toboggan, and many others.

5.  Native American tribal colleges were established to preserve history being lost in oral tradition and colonization. Some of the colleges are only for specific tribes in their territories, while there are quite a few intended for anyone who claims Native American ancestry.

6. The Indian Civil Rights Act of 1968 was passed by Congress to allow Native Americans recourse when in disputes with tribal governments, who were self-governing. It also permitted the US government to intervene in inter-tribal disputes.

7. Native American tribes are mostly self-governing, with the US government allowed to step in only in certain situations. The self-determination movement was afoot for some time before President Nixon recommended in 1970 that they be given more autonomy.

8. Kachina dolls are carved figures usually made of cottonwood root. Their purpose is to teach girls and new brides about katsinas, immortal beings that control certain parts of nature and society, as well as being messengers for humans and spirits.

9. In Florida, the Seminoles refer to their people as "unconquered." They are descendants of three hundred Native Americans, now a population of roughly two thousand. They are most known for refusal to be relocated in the Trail of Tears era. Additionally, as a result of the Seminole Wars, they're the only tribe who never signed a peace treaty with the US government.

10. The Battle of Little Bighorn is also known as "Custer's Last Stand" because, well, he died in it. The Grant

administration intended to take the land of the Sioux in the area and they were refused because it was sacred. The government attacked to force relinquishment, but Custer and all his men were killed.

11. Native Americans are the highest represented group in the US Army, despite being a minority. This has been true since the beginning of the Revolutionary War. Even though Native Americans were not even considered citizens, around twelve-thousand of them volunteered for the Civil War.

12. The travois is a sled that was primarily used by Native Americans to carry goods over large areas of land and helped them to become a more mobile society. It was dragged by hand or with a shoulder harness by dog or horse.

13. Popcorn is a popular snack in the USA but was first discovered by Native Americans in modern Mexico. The Aztecs used it for food, parts of jewelry, and even for divine purposes. Popcorn made its way to the USA and was used as peace offerings and food.

14. Native Americans do not have one set religion; the beliefs vary from tribe to tribe. Generally, their beliefs are lumped together and often leave out the beliefs of smaller tribes.

15. The Navajo Nation is the largest reservation, spreading into parts of Arizona, New Mexico, and Utah. There are currently over 180,000 in their population.

16. The Cherokee were the first Native Americans to be granted US citizenship. They were granted in 1817 due to peace treaty.

17. Other Native Americans weren't afforded citizenship until 1924, which seems odd considering they were here first, but it gets worse. This only applied if they were born in the United States, no matter whether their parents were citizens too, and they didn't have voting rights until 1957.

18. Charles Curtis was Vice President to Herbert Hoover and was most notably the first person with Native American ancestry or even non-European ancestry to reach high office in the executive branch. His mother was a member of the Kaw Nation.

19. Native Americans had a variety of living structures that went well beyond the stereotypical tipi, and at least one influenced other popular traditional styles. The log cabin well known in the United States is an adaptation of the Indian longhouse.

20. Native Americans developed anesthetics long before

the FDA was a twinkle in the US government's eye. They used coca, peyote, and other plants to decrease sensation or consciousness for surgery and pain for centuries before doctors were using anything more than alcohol.

# TEST YOURSELF QUIZ

1. The Pine Ridge Reservation is famous for what significant event?

   A) It's known for its potlatch celebrations.
   B) Ishi came from Pine Ridge.
   C) Custer's Last Stand occurred here.

2. Which Indian tribe received US citizenship a full century before other Native American tribes?

   A) Cherokee

   B) Seminole

   C) Sioux

3. Where did the first people to inhabit the land mass now known as America likely come from?

   A) Europe

   B) Russia

   C) Mexico

4. The Spanish reintroduction of what previously extinct (to the area) animal changed the way Native Americans hunted?

   A) Horse

   B) Dog

   C) Eagle

5. Which of these Native American groups were *not* forcibly relocated on the Trail of Tears?

   A) Creek

   B) Choctaw

   C) Pueblo

**ANSWERS**

1. C
2. A
3. B
4. A
5. C

# CHAPTER TWO

# 1492 — 1783
# COLONIAL HISTORY
# THROUGH THE AMERICAN
# REVOLUTION

Ah, the romanticized years of American history. From the "discovery" of our little piece of paradise by Columbus and through the American Revolution, if not much further into the then-future and even modern times, we've painted a picture of the country's history that isn't completely true. Like the best gossip, it's rooted in truth, but we had to add some details to make it more interesting and leave out the part where we badly misbehaved. It's best to take a light-hearted look at these years, because if we're being honest, the best we can say is, "Thank goodness we've learned from this." Not to make it all sound terrible, Columbus' arrival through the American Revolution covers three centuries of highs that made America great and lows that probably at least made us more powerful.

## In 14-hundred-92, Columbus sailed the ocean blue...

It was a big year for the Spaniards, even if they were a little directionally challenged. Christopher Columbus, Italian explorer and a pretty darn successful colonizer, claimed a good part of the Caribbean for Spain and thus started his work on the Americas. On October 12, he reached the New World, specifically an unidentified island in the Bahamas he called San Salvador. He thought he was in India, so he called the people he found there Indians. He never actually set foot on mainland United States of America, but he gets the credit for it anyway.

Amerigo Vespucci, another Italian explorer, gets naming rights because he proved Columbus wasn't actually in India, which Columbus swore until his death in 1506. Viking Leif Erikson reached Canada 500 years BC—before Columbus's birth, that is—and then there are beliefs that Phoenician sailors were in America in the real BC. Then of course, Native Americans beat them all. No one really knows why Columbus gets the credit, but it makes a nice story. I mean, if we don't mention the genocides and other atrocities he committed or organized.

## The Lost Colony

Now here's a story that was so interesting we couldn't even think of a cool ending. It's a real nail biter at the end. Officially called the Roanoke Colony, the Lost Colony was a settlement on Roanoke Island in North Carolina's Outer Banks, established in 1585 by Queen Elizabeth in an attempt to create an English settlement. One hundred and fifteen settlers lived there for at least two years. These settlers were actually on their way slightly further north to Chesapeake Bay of Virginia, but stopped at Roanoke to pick up a contingent left there the year previously. All they found was a solitary skeleton.

In what was surely a sign of excellent crisis decision-making, they decided not to go to Chesapeake but to settle down on Danger Island instead. (It wasn't called Danger Island, but maybe it should have been, right?) Governor John White attempted to establish relations with the local Native American tribe, the Croatan, but there were difficulties. White eventually left for England to alert to the settlers' struggles on the island and seek supplies. He intended to return quickly, but due to the Anglo-Spanish War, he didn't get back for three years. And much like history rewriting itself, the settlement was deserted—no one left, this time not even a skeleton, but no sign of struggle either. The word "CROATOAN" was carved into a post and "C-R-O" into a tree. All structures had been dismantled, indicating the exit was planned and unrushed. White had instructed the colonists to leave a cross carved into a tree if anything were to happen to them, and no such clue was left. He assumed this meant they had moved on to Croatoan Island (now Hatteras Island) but was unable to search due to massive storms in hurricane season.

Many theories have been posited and investigated. For more than a decade, DNA has even been studied to try to find descendants. There are no known descendants of these settlers and still no answers as to what happened.

## Jamestown

The first permanent English colony was established in 1607 in Jamestown, Virginia. It was chartered by King James I and sponsored by a group of investors who wanted to profit from it. One hundred and four men were the original settlers, with women slowly joining the colony over time. Captain John Smith of Pocahontas fame—though the legend that he married her was false—was the most well-known leader of the colony. Jamestown tried and tried to turn a profit for its investors and always failed, until they started growing tobacco. This was led by John Rolfe, who actually did marry Pocahontas. The legends simply had the wrong John.

29

Tobacco growth was profitable, but Jamestown is historically rather dark in what it represents for the United States, namely the introduction of a harmful product into our gross national product and its acceptance in culture, land grabs of the Powhatan Indians to have enough terrain for tobacco crops, and increased indentured servitude followed by slavery because of increased labor needs.

## The Mayflower

In 1620, the Mayflower transported the first Puritans to the New World, landing at what the 102 Pilgrims called Plymouth Rock. The trip by sea was difficult, but there were only two deaths, which was low for a trans-Atlantic voyage of the time. The New England winter was harsher. The settlers didn't do well on land and stayed on the ship in port for the winter, and over half died in that brief period. Today one in ten Americans are estimated to be descendants of these original colonists.

What history books tell us about the Pilgrims is that they were escaping religious persecution. Actually, they had previously left England for Holland for this reason and were happy with their abilities to practice their religion, according to documents. The problem they found was that in Holland they were losing their sense of English identity, and it was difficult to make a living. They hoped to live free in America, where they could establish society according to standards they saw fit.

## Indian Massacre of 1621

On March 22, 1621, the Powhatans attacked in Virginia, killing 347 men, women, and children, which was a quarter of the population of English colonists in the entire Virginia colony at the time. Jamestown was spared by a last-minute warning, but several villages along the James River were decimated. Spared nearby settlements were abandoned by fearful settlers. The massacre was a result of the first Anglo-Powhatan War, when the English captured Pocahontas. Though Pocahontas married a settler and was released—ensuring a decade of civil relations between the two group—bad blood simmered, and after the Indian group leader's death in 1618, it boiled again under the leadership of a new leader, Pocahontas' uncle, Opchanacanough. After the attack, the Powhatan expected the English to leave, and they let down their guard. In turn, the English used the massacre as moral justification for the next decade to seize Indian land.

Twenty years after the first massacre, another occurred in 1644, this time killing five hundred colonists, but by then that was only a tenth of the population, and the now-older chief was killed. This ultimately led to the decline of the

Powhatan confederacy, of which seven tribes are recognized and only two have retained the reservations of the time of the massacre.

## Giving thanks for racist uncles, a proud tradition

The first Thanksgiving story reminds me of my grandma who taught me "there are three sides to every story—his, hers, and the truth." I wasn't there, so I don't know what really happened, but school children nationwide learn a very sweet tale about two communities who live peacefully side by side in Plymouth—the Wampanoag Indians and Pilgrims. Those Pilgrims, they were really good farmers for being in a new climate on new soil with new plants and had a really bountiful harvest their very first year! So, they invited their neighbors to share. The Pilgrims prepared turkeys they hunted themselves, and the Indians brought deer. They had a three-day celebration, giving thanks for their good fortune and friends. That was in 1621, and ever since, we've celebrated on the fourth Thursday of every November.

The Wampanoag version goes a little differently. The Wampanoag and the Pilgrims had a treaty, and for the most part they lived peacefully—not friendly, but cordially. There actually was a bountiful harvest, thanks to Indians who helped them plant, and the Pilgrims were celebrating by shooting guns into the air. Members of the tribe thought they were preparing for war and went to check it out. The Pilgrims assured them that was not the case, but the Wampanoag camped around the community just to be sure. They left after about three days, accepting it was just a celebration after all.

Kind of a boring story actually, but here's the interesting part: some historians say that the Pilgrim version was never actually told until the nineteenth century, during the Civil War. President Lincoln made it up because families were divided, and he wanted to promote unity. It got people to settle down and enjoy family dinners together. In other words, everyone has a drunk racist uncle we avoid all year until Thanksgiving, and Honest Abe invented the holiday because he felt bad for the poor dude.

## The original Mean Girls

In a small Massachusetts town between February 1692 and May 1693, nineteen men and women were hanged and another seven died in prison, accused of witchcraft in what was known as the Salem Witch Trials. Basically, it was classic bullying turned into hysteria. Some young girls from respectable families accused community outcasts of witchcraft, and the accusations and the tales grew. Typically, someone would have to fall ill and then accuse someone of bewitching them. They may have demonstrated tremors or shaking and accused invisible entities of pinching or abuse in some other fashion. Those who were accused of causing the bewitchment went through legal trials, but the evidence submitted was hardly impartial, including the paranormal and what we'd now have thrown out as "hearsay." Sometimes though, trials didn't occur. The accused were hunted down by mobs and murdered before legal processes could begin.

The stories hold a morbid fascination for most Americans, and over the years there have been many medical and psychological armchair diagnoses considered for the afflictions of those who made accusations. Hysteria in response to Indian attacks, convulsions caused by eating infected rye bread, a bird-borne encephalitis epidemic, and sleep paralysis have all been posited. Modern theories seem to lean more toward meanness, though. Without evidence of medical cause and a little more insight into human psychology, the trending belief is more along the lines of spite and attention-seeking behaviors.

## The Great Awakening

This Protestant religious revival spread throughout British America and Europe in the 1730s, leaving an impact that is still felt today. It divided the people and split up congregations, with many beginning their own churches and schools as they parted ways with their congregation's teachings. It was a movement that made religion deeply personal to people and connected with them, encouraging an introspection and personal reflection on morality that hadn't previously been a focus. It was a break from the impersonal ritual and ceremony of previous Christianity and resulted from the powerful evangelistic-style preaching that was popular in the time and rises again today. Particularly evident in New England Protestantism and in the South amongst slaves and free blacks, it gave rise to the Baptist sect of Christianity.

While in many ways stifling to women and minorities, the Great Awakening also indirectly led to the free thought and independence fostered in people and eventually birthed ideas that gradually gave more rights to women and blacks in America. Some of the first published writings from non-white, non-male Americans without the use of pseudonyms came in the form of at least partially spirituality-based musings during this period.

## French-Indian War

From 1754 to 1763, the colonies fought against New France, located from modern-day Newfoundland to the Canadian midland, from the Hudson Bay to the Gulf of

Mexico and including all the Great Lakes. They both had military from their respective European origin countries, and different Indian federations fought on both sides; the British army far outnumbered the French and the French relied heavily on Indian assistance. Even so, the British side trumped the French four to one and declared victory in America, where fighting was mostly over by 1760. It continued in Europe until the Treaty of Paris, with the British as victors and gaining several territories. The debt Britain incurred led to their enactment of the Tea Act, which then led to the Revolutionary War.

## The Boston Massacre

On March 5, 1770, the British Army in Boston found themselves under attack by a mob and shot into the crowd without orders, killing five and injuring six. Civilians instigated a quarrel with the British soldiers, and the soldiers made the poor decision to respond, escalating the event. Crowds swelled, and church bells were rung to alert others. Witness accounts say that civilians grew violent first, pushing and throwing rocks, but of course, they did not carry the firepower the soldiers did, and the frightened soldiers forgot their training and opened fire.

Patriot activists like Paul Revere criticized the incident heavily and encouraged rebellion against the British. The mobs as a result of the massacre led the army to retreat, and eight soldiers, an officer, and four civilians were arrested and charged with murder. They were defended by John Adams, interestingly a future President, and most went free. Historically, the incident is attributed to causing the American Revolution, in part, helping to turn colonists against King George III and British authority.

## Boston Tea Party

The Sons of Liberty, led by Samuel Adams, organized this historic political protest on December 16, 1773. It is arguably the most defining protest of the country's existence and was in defiance of the Tea Act, which the protesters believed was taxation without representation. They had to pay taxes on the imported tea. The activists, dressed as Mohawk Indians, boarded ships and threw an entire shipment of tea into the Boston Harbor. The British government was not at all pleased, and this event in large part led to the Revolutionary War. One of Great Britain's retaliatory responses was The Coercive Acts, which shut down Boston commerce and revoked Massachusetts' authority for self-governance. Not just Massachusetts, but all thirteen colonies, responded in anger and convened the First Continental Congress, petitioning the monarchy for repeal, which they of course denied. And thus began the war.

## The British are coming!

On April 18th, 1775, Paul Revere rode horseback through Concord, Massachusetts, warning "The British are coming! The British are coming!" He saved the day—the country actually—by warning Colonial forces of the British army's impending arrival, and the next day the American Revolutionary War began with the Battles of Lexington and Concord. More than two hundred people were killed, but it wasn't the complete massacre it would have been if Revere hadn't been able to warn others.

That's the story anyway, but you may have already figured out that America's greatest legacy is our gift for storytelling. Revere was actually with two other men, Samuel Prescott and William Dawes, and they set out with the intent of warning of the invasion, but they were detained by British patrols. Prescott managed to escape, and he did go to Concord, warning the townsfolk to hide ammunition and weapons. Dawes got away later, but he followed in the footsteps of Columbus and got lost in the dark. Revere was released without his horse later in the night and walked back to Lexington to warn them... that a battle was going to begin hours ago. The first shots were fired while he was in captivity. Well, he meant well.

## The first Independence Day

On July 4, 1776, the Declaration of Independence was adopted after having been agreed to two days prior. On this day, our Founders officially regarded themselves as a new nation and no longer British. Actually though, for it to be "official" took months, perhaps years. It seems legally binding signatures made some Founding Fathers a little nervous. It was the agreed-to day though, and it was the date on the copies distributed through the colonies.

You might find it hard to believe, but the first Independence Day didn't have a lot of fireworks and hot dogs on the grill, and no bikinis on the beach. There may have been some beer, as several of them were brewers. That detail has been left out of the traditional retelling. Instead, they sat in a stifling room and argued, probably. Thomas Jefferson wrote the majority, and Benjamin Franklin and John Adams helped with the editing process. The most famous line of the document says, "We hold these truths to be self-evident, that all men are created equal, that they are endowed by their Creator with certain unalienable rights, that among those are Life, Liberty, and the pursuit of Happiness."

There were 56 signers, the delegates from the thirteen colonies known as the Second Continental Congress. Have you ever heard someone ask for your John Hancock? That means they want you to sign something. It's slang for a signature, because John Hancock was a signer with a very distinctive signature. It was certainly beautiful, and it was large. He happened to be the first signer, and when someone commented on how big it was, he responded—so the story goes—that he wanted King George III to be able to read it without his glasses. Historical accuracy be damned! It's a cute story, but as it turns out, he just has a really large signature. It's the same on all the documents he signed.

## Treaty of Paris

The Treaty of Paris ended the Revolutionary War and recognized American Independence from Great Britain. It was signed in Paris on September 3, 1783, and gave America land to the Mississippi River and up to Canada. While America was given its independence, provisions required American payment of debts to British citizens and called for fair treatment of British loyalists in the former colonies. Many of the loyalists remained, but eighty thousand left for Canada and the West Indies or headed back to Great Britain. They had been treated as enemies during the war, with property and civil rights taken. The British compensated many loyalists, and after a generation, those who stayed in America were indistinguishable from other Americans.

# An overview of slavery

Jamestown, Virginia, was the first site of African slave arrival and trade in 1619. Dutch traders had actually seized them from a captured Spanish slave ship. Settlers needed assistance with crop production, especially tobacco, as necessary farming labor exceeded their ability. Indians were enslaved too, though on a smaller scale. The economy of the colonies relied heavily on slavery. In fact, it was crucial.

Massachusetts was the first colony to codify indentured servitude, saying that it was legal if they were purchased somewhere else, among a few other legal bases. The United States Constitution protected slavery, but in the late 18th century, an abolition movement picked up steam.

Slaves were mistreated and of course uncompensated for their hard work, but they were also violently abused from whippings to hangings, with burnings and mutilations in between. Some 12.5 million slaves were shipped from Africa to the New World, with about two million dying en route and the majority going to Brazil and the Caribbean. Four percent came to what is now the United States. There are no numbers for how many babies were born into slavery, but young women were advertised as good breeding stock and sold at higher prices. Some owners promised freedom once a woman gave birth to fifteen children, and at least one slave trader advertised of "breeding practices" that helped him sell six thousand slave children every year.

# INTERESTING FACTS

1.  The Niña, the Pinta, and the Santa Maria were the ships in Christopher Columbus' armada for his voyage to the New World. The Pinta was the fastest, the Niña was the strongest—having already been the sole survivor of one hurricane in a previous voyage with another fleet—and the Santa Maria was the largest.

2.  The first Thanksgiving didn't include our "traditional" foods like turkey, sweet potatoes, or cranberries. Goose or duck was the more likely game, sweet potatoes weren't grown yet, and sugar was too much of a luxury for cranberries. The meal probably included pumpkin, succotash, and corn.

3.  The first Treaty of Paris, in 1763, declared an end to the French and Indian War, and France gave up its mainland America territories, ensuring that it was no longer a military threat to the British colonies. Spain gave Florida to Britain, and Britain gave Cuba to them.

4.  All the old pals met again in Paris twenty years later, a reunion this time to talk about old times and sign the second Treaty of Paris, in which King George III and representatives from America declared an end to the

Revolutionary War.

5. Thomas Paine wrote his pamphlet *Common Sense* in January 1776, encouraging a break from Britain. The proportion of people who read it is equivalent to those who watch the Super Bowl every year in modern times. Not bad since the internet wasn't as popular back then.

6. Deborah Sampson dressed as a man so that she could serve in the Continental Army during the Revolutionary War. She is the only woman to have earned a military pension for serving.

7. The British are theater people, no matter what! They gave the world Shakespeare, and they gave America Broadway—sort of. When the British Army occupied New York City, they set up theaters, acted in their downtime, and the public attended their plays. So basically, a colonist on the battlefield might have put down his musket and said, "You look familiar. Don't I know you from somewhere?" To which the Brit may have replied, "That depends, did you attend Othello three nights ago in New York City?" 'Ah, yes! Your performance as Iago was brilliant!" And then they shot each other.

8. The Magna Carta is an eight-hundred-year-old document that inspired the Constitution of the United

States, establishing that everyone, even rulers or political leaders, is subject to the law and establishing individual rights including justice and fair trial.

9. The Declaration of Independence states that "all men are created equal," but what is intended by the term "all men" is a point of contention. Generally believed to have been a generic term for "humanity", as the word "men" or "man" is still sometimes used, some have claimed it intentionally excluded women and children. Others point out that the Founding Fathers were slave owners, and it likely only meant white people, or just white men.

10. King George III is known as "the king who went mad and lost America." Modern historians and psychiatrists believe he may have actually suffered from bipolar disorder, unheard of then. He came to the throne at a rather tumultuous time, and Minister George Grenville was responsible for the Stamp Act that eventually led to the Revolutionary War.

11. The first two drafts of the Declaration of Independence were supposedly written on hemp paper. The final version, still in existence and on display, was written on parchment. This is actually urban myth, but it may be true, as hemp paper was common back then. The

drafts don't exist for evidence, and we are almost positive that is not because the Founding Fathers smoked it.

12. The Liberty Bell is one of the most iconic symbols of American history. The bell could be heard all over Philadelphia, the nation's capital at the time, but despite the stories, it did not ring on July 4, 1776. It likely did ring, along with others all over town, on July 8, to mark the reading of the Declaration of the Independence.

13. The word "independence" is not used once in the Declaration of Independence other than the title. The last word in the document is "honor."

14. George Washington owned one of the largest whiskey distilleries in America. You can actually tour his still-operational distillery on the grounds of Mount Vernon.

15. Washington set a high standard for farewell addresses with the letter published near the end of his second term in the newspaper American Daily Advertiser. One nugget of wisdom was that a moral, enlightened nation must be educated. He said, "In proportion as the structure of a government gives force to public opinion, it is essential that public opinion should be enlightened." In other words, if you know anyone who

can't name the current President, tell them Voting Day is on a Saturday.

16. Patrick Henry was a Founding Father, attorney, and orator. He famously cried, "Give me liberty, or give me death!" when asking for military intervention in Jamaica, which was experiencing British interference. If you study his portraits, you may find yourself unsure as to which option he ultimately chose.

17. Alexander Hamilton was so colorful a character, he is now memorialized in a Broadway show bearing his name. He had a rough childhood. His mother met his father while she was fleeing an abusive husband. Because he was illegitimate, society of the time labeled him a bastard and "son of a whore." His father later abandoned them, and she died when Alexander was still a child. He largely educated himself, though he was taken in by a wealthy family, and he served in the military, becoming Washington's aide and going on to become a Founding Father.

18. Manifest Destiny was the nineteenth century idea that Americans were destined by God to control the entire American continent. This belief is what inspired western expansion, Indian removal, and war with Mexico. The concept began with President Andrew

Jackson, but the term came from a reporter who was a follower of the president.

19. James Madison may have been the most accomplished of all the very, very impressive Founding Fathers. He wrote the first drafts of the United States Constitution, and he co-wrote the Federalist Papers. He sponsored the Bill of Rights, which holds the first ten amendments to the Constitution. He established the Democrat-Republican party with then-President Thomas Jefferson, and later became president himself in 1808. He was a case of really growing into his destiny, as at the first Constitutional Convention he was known for being one of the youngest and most reserved men present.

20. Sixteenth century America is frequently referred to as "The Lost Years" because school history books (and indeed, scholarly texts as well) don't mention the century-plus that occurred between 1492 and the settlement of Jamestown in 1607. However, there were Spanish-based and French-based communities in the southwest and southeast long before the Puritans. In fact, St. Augustine, FL was founded in the late sixteenth century and is the oldest European settlement in the nation.

# TEST YOURSELF

1. Who was the first signer of the Declaration of Independence?

   A) John Hancock
   B) George Washington
   C) Thomas Jefferson

2. Where did Christopher Columbus think he had landed when he discovered America?

   A) The West Indies
   B) India
   C) Spain

3. Where was the nation's first capital?

   A) Boston
   B) Washington, D.C.
   C) Philadelphia

4. Which state was the first to codify indentured servitude?

   A) Massachusetts
   B) North Carolina
   C) Arizona

5. Thomas Paine wrote what historic bestseller?

   A) *Sense & Sensibility*
   B) *Common Sense*
   C) *Pride & Prejudice*

## ANSWERS

1. A
2. B
3. C
4. A
5. B

# CHAPTER THREE

# 1783 — 1918
# AMERICAN INDEPENDENCE
# TO WORLD WAR I

From the end of the American Revolution to World War I, the United States went through a period of development which, if likened to a child's, could best be described as growing pains. As a nation, it struggled with the morality of past sins and the promise of future progress, but was on its way to establishing itself as a world power at the same time. It's a tricky tightrope to balance upon, making immoral situations right while trying to maintain the forward momentum that abuse of power originally gave you. It appears to still be a work in progress, but as you'll see when studying the growth of the United States of America from revolution to the First World War, for some time certainly they were on the right track.

## End of Revolutionary War

The fight for US independence was far more prolonged than either the British or American sides had anticipated. What started with the appearance of assured rapid victory for Great Britain's superior military training, became by 1778 a global conflict that spread into the North Sea, the Caribbean, Prussia, Central America, and even India as international players entered the conflict in support of either American colonists or the British Crown.

Most of the fighting on US soil occurred east of the Appalachians, with the New England and mid-Atlantic states especially devastated in the early years, and the southern colonies hit hard later over eight years of siege. A series of blunders by British generals, especially those committed by Howe in the Philadelphia Campaign, and judgment errors by Cornwallis in Yorktown, and unexpected victories by American colonist forces in other key locations such as Saratoga, precipitated foreign support of the American movement.

Most notably, Prussian and French support of additional troops, supplies, training, and equipment started turning the tide of the war, and several key surrenders on the varied battle fronts occurred between 1778 and 1791. Finally, after 104 months of fighting, the "Peace of Paris" was signed on

September 3, 1793, whereby King George III of Britain formally recognized the independence of the American colonies. One out of every sixteen men of military age were killed in the war.

## Alien and Sedition Acts

Some of the most controversial laws the US ever enacted, the Alien and Sedition Acts of 1798, were signed into law by John Adams, acting under pressure from a Federalist-dominated Congress. The Alien Acts were directed against immigrants and others deemed non-nationals, making it harder for immigrants to gain citizenship, allowing for deportation of noncitizens who were classified as "dangerous", and allowing for deportation of any person in the US who was from a nation deemed hostile. The Sedition Act criminalized the making of purported false criticism of the federal government.

The socially conservative Federalists made the argument that the acts improved national security during a time of undeclared war; their opponents and critics argued that they were about suppression of voters and silencing of dissent. Thomas Jefferson allowed most to expire during his term, but the Alien Enemy Act was never repealed and was modified and invoked by US president Franklin D. Roosevelt to imprison US resident aliens of Japanese,

Italian, and German descent during World War II, and then again by President Truman after hostilities ended to conduct deportations of persons of those origins. This act is still on the books, meaning that its broad application could be invoked again.

## Monroe Doctrine

In 1823, many territories under colonial control in the North and South American continents had achieved, or were fighting for, independence, mainly from Spain and Portugal. Wanting to completely separate "Old World" and "New World" spheres of influence, President James Monroe issued a policy opposing any new European colonization of independent states in the Americas.

Known as the Monroe Doctrine, by 1850 the policy declared that any new attempt by a European power to take control of any independent state in the region would be viewed as "manifestation of an unfriendly disposition towards the United States." Existing European colonies were still recognized, and the US announced a policy of non-interference with European internal affairs.

President Monroe announced the policy in the January 1823 State of the Union address. In hindsight, the doctrine has been seen as one of the most definitive moments of US foreign policy, as well as one of its longest standing policies.

## Petticoat Affair

In the long history of US Presidents, there has never been any shortage of scandals, either within the administrations, or, apparently, among their spouses. The Petticoat Affair was one famous example of behavior more fitting perhaps to today's high school settings than to the offices of national leadership. In hindsight, the attitudes underlying the incident were very important to the launching of the women's suffrage and rights movements.

Andrew Jackson's Secretary of War, John Eaton, married his wife, Peggy, a few months after Peggy's first husband had passed away, a move seen to be in violation of existing "moral standards of decency" at the time. This, plus the fact that Peggy was seen as an outspoken woman seeking influence in the political and world stage, brought to the surface an underlying fear of social disruption and inevitable change.

The wife of Vice-President Calhoun, Floride, led the other cabinet wives, the "petticoats," in what was essentially a complete campaign of social ostracism that prevented the Eatons' participation in just about every social event as a rebuke to Peggy's perceived character flaws. Jackson backed the Eatons during the events, and the scandal led to the resignation of almost the entire cabinet. The long-term downstream effect was a division in US society regarding the role of women in professional, personal, and political spheres, and the emergence of the roots of modern feminism.

## Seneca Falls

In an age in which we can turn on the television in the United States and see scores of prominent and outspoken women, it's easy to forget that US women once were often not allowed to even speak in public. A group of women in Seneca Falls, NY, held a convention in 1848 to start changing that. Organized by Elizabeth Cady Stanton and a group of regional Quaker women, the convention attracted three hundred attendees from July 19-20 to discuss the "social, civil, and religious condition and rights of women."

Stanton and the other organizers had prepared a Declaration of Sentiments and a list of accompanying resolutions which included the right to vote, the most intensely debated item on the list. The only African American in attendance at the conference, Frederick Douglass, encouraged the inclusion of suffrage in the resolutions, and it stayed. The Declaration of Sentiments became the guiding document for the emergence of the women's rights movement, which has sought ever since to provide women with the same rights as men in the US.

## California gold rush

After the Mexican-American War led to the annexation of the geographically rich and diverse territory of California, the region was mostly sparsely populated by people struggling to adapt to the changed status of nationality and governance. Then, on January 24, 1848, a prospector named James Marshall discovered gold in a stream at Sutter's Mill in Coloma, California. The news of Sutter's discovery spread very rapidly, and a rush of 300,000 migrants from the rest of the continental US and all over the world flocked to California seeking their fortune in gold.

From 1848 to 1855, gold worth tens of billions of dollars was discovered and flowed into the struggling US economy, stabilizing it. California was made a state before it was ever a colony, in 1850. Agriculture, ranching, and other services that met demands for burgeoning population growth boomed. The city of San Francisco went from two hundred settlers in 1848 to 36,000 by 1855. The lack of laws regarding property rights for mining operations had devastating effects on the existing Native and Mexican California populations, and many succumbed to disease, genocide, starvation, and property theft.

Approximately half of the settlers who arrived for the Gold Rush arrived by land from across the continent; the rest arrived by ship across or up the Latin American coast from the Pacific. The need to move people and supplies rapidly spurred the development of the Transcontinental Railroad connecting the west and east coasts in 1849, and many technological advances were made during the same period that were directly related to or financed by the gold of California.

## Fugitive Slave Act of 1850

By the mid-1850s, slavery was an unstable institution, and there was little incentive for escaped slaves to be returned to the South, whose economy was dependent on their work. Southern politicians put a great pressure on the US government to penalize authorities who did not assist the return of escaped slaves, and after a series of skirmishes, the Fugitive Slave Act of 1850 was enacted. The law forced the hand by fining those who did not aid the return of suspected fugitive slaves.

Some states challenged the law and extended protections to escaped slaves in their borders. This angered Southern states and set the stage for the secession that would fuel the

Civil War. Abolitionists went into open revolt. Through all of this, the North realized that complete abolition of slavery was a necessary and key tenet of policy for the looming war over secession. Laws were passed by the North in rapid succession to completely negate the spirit and letter of the Fugitive Slave Act.

## Emancipation Proclamation

The January 1, 1863, Emancipation Proclamation was a direct war measure issued by President Lincoln. It freed all slaves in lands under Confederate control and was issued without Congressional approval. Although large slave-owning territories were not covered by the Proclamation, it did apply to three million—75 percent—of the slaves in American lands. Any slave that escaped control of the Confederate government was immediately free. Persons considered suitable for armed service, could, upon freedom, immediately conscript as paid soldiers and personnel in the armed forces. There was no compensation for slave owners, and freed slaves were not granted immediate citizenship, nor was slavery explicitly outlawed by the act.

However, the proclamation changed the nature of the dialogue of the Civil War, from one of states' rights to one specifically moving towards abolishment of slavery. Slaves living in Union territories and those under Union control were freed with the Thirteenth Amendment after the Civil War, or, in some cases, by states themselves during or before the war. The proclamation led to the immediate freeing of between 25,000 to 75,000 slaves in regions where the US Army was active, and as Union forces advanced, did lead to the gradual emancipation of the rest of three million in the covered region.

## 1906 earthquake

In the early morning of April 18, 1906, the San Andreas fault line experienced two major ruptures, the stronger evaluated later after invention of the Richter scale as being between a 7.8 and 8.3 magnitude, with the epicenter most likely located just off the San Francisco coast. The earthquake caused the complete devastation of San Francisco and nearby cities, with 80 percent of San Francisco destroyed and an estimated seven hundred to three thousand immediate deaths attributed to the initial impact. As many as 300,000 people were left homeless, living in tent cities for as long as two years.

The quake had permanent impacts, both on the surrounding terrain and on US-conscience. The initial collapses and resulting massive structural fires led to the reorganization of the city, allowing for more livability, and creating the modern zoning and layout the city is known for today. Los

Angeles picked up the port traffic that San Francisco lost, becoming the new trade center of power for the West Coast. The earthquake was one of the first large-scale natural disasters for which the US government issued a national level response (although it was inadequate to cover the needs). Large individual donors, private citizens, and foreign entities reached out with substantial support.

The quake also pushed great advances in scientific discovery and in geologic understanding for building zoning and safety standards in construction, as well as fueling new frontiers in the insurance industry.

## Girl Scouts and Boy Scouts of America

The Boy Scouts of America began in 1910, two years after its origin in Great Britain. Soon it was the nation's largest youth organization, although it has been steeped in periodic controversies nearly since its inception. The organization often resists change reflected in society as it leans toward traditionalism. For example, since its start, it has allowed boys of color to participate in programming but stated that local troops may follow rules of local schools. Since schools were segregated in that era, troops were "separate but equal" for decades.

Girl scouting has proven just as popular, beginning in 1912

with eighteen members and having 3.7 million in present day. Facing the same controversies, Girl Scouts have a pattern of facing the backlash earlier, as they have been more proactive to adopt change. Either way, both Boy Scouts and Girl Scouts have been instrumental in American society since their start, with almost all children from the last few generations either being active members at some point during their childhood or wishing to be.

## World War I

The War to End All Wars began in 1914 and ended near the end of 1918. Sixty million European and ten million other world military personnel engaged in battle, with more than ten percent killed along with seven million civilians. It involved every established or emerging economic world super power split into two factions—Germany and Austria-Hungary versus the Allied forces of Great Britain, France, and the Russian Empire. The United States entered in 1917 under President Wilson's leadership, after Wilson had attempted to keep the US out of the conflict, including a failed attempt to negotiate a peace treaty.

World War I was the United States' first use of a military draft, with less than fifty thousand armed forces but a need for more than a million. Though Americans had fewer forces in the war, they were instrumental in the surrender of the German forces. In September, the US aided the French in an attack against the Germans and took more than 25,000 troops as prisoners. A month later, they had to surrender.

There were a great many effects of the war on home life in the United States, but one of the biggest shifts was in the changing roles of women. Men left their jobs to join the war effort, and women had no income while jobs sat vacant. It was the first time large numbers of women began careers so that they could feed their families and the economy wouldn't stagnate with no workers. World War I had many implications, both positive and negative, in the United States and other nations, but that has been one of the biggest and longest lasting.

## National park system

In 1916, President Wilson signed the Organic Act, creating the National Park Services, to be overseen by the Department of the Interior and responsible for protecting United States' national parks and monuments. The first of these parks was established in 1872, and you may have heard it. It's a little place called Yellowstone National Park. Interestingly, the system is the first of its kind and set off a worldwide movement, with more than half of the world's nations now having some sort of similar programming and more than 1,200 parks. By the time the Organic Act came to fruition, there were 35 parks, and now there are more than four hundred over 84 million acres in every state, district, and territory. There are now twenty thousand employees who protect local and national history.

## First Red Scare

Early twentieth century events surrounding the Russian Revolution and its effect on the world stage created what was known as the Red Scare in the US—widespread fear of Communism and anarchism, whether warranted or not. By 1919-1920, almost all emerging organized labor and union movements were affected by the general sense of paranoia that infiltrated society. All worker's rights activity tended to get labeled, often erroneously, as Communistic or anarchistic in nature, and use of deadly force against early labor leaders and activists was justified through anti-Communist language. A series of anarchistic bombings cemented the fear into action, and US Attorney General A. Mitchell Palmer spearheaded a campaign of exaggerated, increased violent and suppressive rhetoric, illegal searches and seizures, arrests and detentions conducted without a warrant, and the deportation of hundreds of suspected "radicals."

At the same time, US society saw a growing nationalistic and nativism movement, directed especially against immigrants from Eastern and Southern Europe, citing fear of Communist influence as an excuse for discrimination. The scare came and went quickly but also left its seeds in the US psyche for distrust of organized rights movements in general and for later support of international policies curbing the global spread of Communism.

## Women's suffrage movement

The women's suffrage movement began picking up steam after the 1848 Seneca Falls convention, and more than seventy years later, women were granted the right to vote with the ratification of the Nineteenth Amendment in 1920. This was two years after the end of World War I, which changed the way women were viewed in society. Contributions to the war effort challenged the ideas of mental and physical inferiority and made it clear that it could no longer be argued women were unfit to vote. If they could keep munitions factories open and men at war properly armed for defense, then they could surely choose conscientiously in a voting booth.

## Public schools movement

The American Revolution brought on the first free public schools, but the movement particularly began to grow in the mid-nineteenth century, as there became a need to better educate growing former slave populations who had not had formal education previously. States began passing laws making school compulsory and used federal funding to establish colleges in agriculture and engineering. By 1870, every state had free elementary schools, at least in their urban centers. By 1892, educators recommended twelve years of schooling—eight years in elementary with four years of high school—and a few years later, high school and higher education standards were being developed as well. By 1910, 72 percent of children attended school, and by 1930, almost all were enrolled in schools, excluding children with significant disabilities.

# INTERESTING FACTS

1. Eli Whitney's 1794 invention of the cotton gin created massive growth in cotton production in the South, where production quadrupled in twenty years. It sped up the process of separating seeds from the fiber, but rather than promote greater ease of work, greed got in the way, and it made the region more dependent on slavery as they demanded greater profit. By 1860, American slaves produced two-thirds of the world's cotton.

2. The Naturalization Act of 1795 specified that anyone wishing to become a naturalized United States citizen must be free and white, and in eliminating most of the first qualifications for applicants of the time, also required "good moral character." Sorry, slaveowners, I guess you were disqualified. Office poll: Does "good moral character" mean anyone who pushed for naturalization to be white-only had their citizenship stripped? We found the catch-22.

3. We thought twenty-first-century politics were nasty, but in 1804, former vice-president Aaron Burr killed Alexander Hamilton, everyone's favorite dancing and

singing statesman, in a duel. The duel was an escalation of years of animosity between the men, and Hamilton had almost succeeded at taking Burr down completely. Duels were somewhat socially acceptable ways to handle grievances at the time, but Hamilton was well-loved, and Burr's career was destroyed.

4.  The Oregon Trail extends from the Missouri River in Kansas all the way to Oregon. Generation Xer's know it best as where they died of dysentery in green block letters in elementary school libraries across the nation, but even more importantly, this was the land mapped by Lewis and Clark while exploring unsettled America west of the Missouri.

5.  In a move that surprises no one, the Bureau of Indian Affairs was created without authorization by Secretary of War Calhoun in 1824. One of the most abhorrent things the office did (in a long, long list) was to educate native children in boarding schools, assimilating and prohibiting them from speaking in their language or practicing their religion or other cultural traditions.

6.  Thomas Jefferson and John Adams died exactly fifty years to the day after they signed the Declaration of Independence. They were long-time friends but

occasional rivals, and Adams last words were supposedly "Thomas Jefferson survives." He didn't know that his friend had just died five hundred miles away. It's unconfirmed, but I like to imagine this utterance as full of lament because he wanted to roast Jefferson good at his funeral. However, I suspect they hugged it out at the pearly gates.

7. In 1831, a young slave named Nat Turner led a revolt freeing slaves, gathering horses and guns, and calling for people to join. He freed about seventy people, but there were 55 eventually executed, including Turner, and white militias killed 120 blacks, most of whom were not involved.

8. On February 25, 1835, Samuel Colt received his patent for a rotating cylinder revolver design that allowed a gun to be shot multiple times without reload. The Colt Paterson was the clumsy precursor to modern guns, and Colt died one of the richest men in America for his invention.

9. Harriet Beecher Stowe, teacher and abolitionist, wrote an anti-slavery novel Abraham Lincoln attributed to "starting the war." *Uncle Tom's Cabin* sold 300,000 copies in the United States alone (in Britain it sold a million; I guess they were laughing at how badly we

messed up this revolution thing). While it was certainly historically valuable, it's controversial and a favorite of many (this author included), while criticized for popularizing stereotypes. "Uncle Tom", for example, today is considered a slur.

10. The Dred Scott Decision was a fascinatingly hopeless and hypocritical Supreme Court case in which a slave tried to fight for his family's freedom in 1857, stating that because he had lived in territories where slavery was illegal, he could not be held in Missouri. The Court decided that he did not have right to bring federal suit because people with African ancestry were not citizens, nor did his temporary residence outside of Missouri matter because it would improperly deprive his owner of property. Interestingly, the case did lead in a roundabout way to his freedom, but sadly he died a year later of tuberculosis.

11. The Pony Express was the United States mail system for eighteen months from 1860 to 1861. It didn't last, but it's an iconic part of American history. Mail was delivered 1,800 miles in ten days, with 157 stations about ten miles apart from one another, extending from Missouri to California.

12. The secession of 1860 to 1861 occurred when eleven

states joined to form the Confederate States of America, and it brought on the Civil War. The southern states cried for states' rights because they were economically dependent on slavery while an abolition movement was growing and threatening livelihood. The Confederacy lost, and a surprising number of Americans are still bitter about it.

13. We have a long tradition in the US of blaming "Mrs. O'Leary's cow" when we don't want to admit making a mistake. It's origin? It's a reference to the tragic Great Chicago Fire of October 10, 1871. Three hundred people died, 100,000 residents were made homeless, and more than three square miles of the city was destroyed. No one really knows how it started, but we know it was in a barn owned by the O'Leary family. A popular tale is that her cow knocked over a lantern with its tail.

14. In 1876, the first version of Major League Baseball was founded. Professional baseball had come around five years earlier with another league, but it was mismanaged and quickly disbanded. The National League, and later the American League, which both play in the MLB today, made baseball America's number one pastime.

15. The telephone was invented by Alexander Graham Bell in 1876, and the lightbulb in 1879 by Thomas Alva Edison. If there a celebrity death match to decide which one was more important to Americans, the phone would win. But then how would you charge it?

16. The O.K. Corral lives in American infamy for an 1881 thirty-second shootout between a group of outlaws and lawmen in Tombstone, Arizona. The gunfight was the culmination of a feud between five cowboys on one side and lawmen Doc Holliday and the Earp brothers on the other. The cowboys were tired of the Earps' interference in their criminal enterprises, and the lawmen were tired of death threats. Two of the tough guys ran away, and the other three were killed. Funny that our history glorifies this lawless time when modern gangs strike a little more fear in our hearts.

17. James Naismith gave the world the gift of basketball in 1891, founding the University of Kansas program, taking the sport to the Olympics, and training other great coaching legends. He was Canadian-American and worked as both a coach and a physician.

18. Galveston, Texas, holds the unfortunate record of having hosted in 1900 the worst hurricane and possibly worst natural disaster in United States history, with

even low estimates of eight thousand deaths being more than all other hurricanes since. There were so many bodies that they had to be burned in funeral pyres and buried at sea, and whiskey was passed out to the traumatized men who had to collect the bodies.

19. North Carolina is first in flight, but the Wright Brothers who piloted the flight were from Ohio. They ran a bike shop, and in tinkering with pieces came up with a plan for a flyer. They decided to test it in Kill Devil Hills, North Carolina, in 1903 because the area was private, with steady winds and wide, open spaces. They sought weather data from the US Weather Bureau, then wrote to the locations that fit their criteria. Kill Devil Hills had the friendliest, most welcoming reply.

20. RMS Titanic was a 1912 cruise ship from Great Britain that sank in the North Atlantic after hitting an iceberg. More than 1,500 people died, but it would have been 1,499 if Rose had let Jack onto the door. Actually, that's a fictional story, though Americans obsess over it more than the fascination with the voyage itself. Other interesting REAL facts about the ship: Its architect and commander both went down with the ship, and some of the wealthiest people in the world were aboard.

# TEST YOURSELF

1. Who invented the cotton gin?

   A) Thomas Alva Edison
   B) Samuel Colt
   C) Eli Whitney

2. What was the name of the first US National Park to open?

   A) Yellowstone National Park
   B) Yosemite National Park
   C) Joshua Tree National Park

3. Which was invented first, baseball or basketball?

   A) Basketball
   B) Baseball
   C) Basketball was invented first, but baseball went professional first.

4. What was Floride Calhoun's argument with Peggy Eaton referred to as?

   A) The Petty Affair
   B) The Petticoat Affair
   C) The War to End All Wars

5. When was the United States' first use of military draft?

   A) Revolutionary War

   B) Civil War

   C) World War I

## ANSWERS

1. C
2. A
3. B
4. B
5. C

# CHAPTER FOUR

# 1918 – 1964
# WORLD WAR I
# TO CIVIL RIGHTS

From World War I to the Civil Rights Movement era in 1964, the United States experienced some the highs and the lows of unpredictability that come with being a world leader. While experiencing relative prosperity in this time, the United States was also the catalyst in the worldwide Great Depression. If you've ever wondered what effect your country could possibly have on another unless engaged in active war, you're invited to study the Great Depression and the years before and after in great detail. Still, the United States and the world itself recovered, and there were other wrongs to rectify and battles to fight.

## Treaty of Versailles

Signed in 1918, the Treaty of Versailles signaled the end of World War I and the armistice that would not only bring about reparations for the countries affected by Germany's wrath, but—a lesser discussed fact in your high school history classes—secure regulation of the drug trade around the world. The treaty was signed by Germany, the United States, France, China, the United Kingdom, Japan, Italy, Persia, the Netherlands, Portugal, Russia, and Siam.

The international opium convention was formed under the covenant of the League of Nations, and its primary goal was to control and regulate the opium, cocaine, and India Hemp drug trades. Germany gave the trademarks for aspirin and heroin to France, Britain, Russia, and the United States as part of the war reparations.

## Nineteenth Amendment

When the United States of America adopted its constitution, it left suffrage undefined on a national level because it required the states to define the qualifications for the voter. As a result, white men held the exclusive voting power for some time, with black men being extended the right much later. During the late 1800s, a few territories began recognizing women's right to vote and initiated plans to introduce legislation to the United States Congress in 1878.

After more than thirty years of little to no success, the tireless efforts of women's suffrage aligned themselves with movements of change during the 1912 election. Momentum gained, and on August 18, 1920, the federal government finally adopted the ratification of the Nineteenth Amendment, allowing women the right to vote.

## Scopes Trial

Tennessee v. Scopes, also known as the Scopes Monkey Trial, was a pretty fascinating legal case in 1925. A substitute teacher named John Scopes violated the Butler Act, banning the teaching of human evolution in state schools.

If that's not strange enough for you, it was deliberately staged to attract attention to the town of Dayton. Scopes couldn't remember if he actually taught any evolution, but he incriminated himself to provide a defendant for the state. While this obviously turned a serious issue into a spectacle, the pot-stirrers got what they wanted. Scopes was fined, the Tennessee Supreme Court upheld the statute (which was repealed by the state legislature in 1967), and Dayton certainly got the attention it sought.

## Great Depression

The Great Depression began the day the US stock market collapsed on Black Tuesday, October 29, 1929. Economic security spiraled for four years as the gross domestic product decreased by fifteen percent, and before the bottom hit in 1933, the unemployment rate reached 25 percent. Many theorists have weighed in on the causes of the Great Depression, and none so widely accepted and critiqued as the "boom and bust" theory that unbalanced accumulation of wealth during industrialization in capitalism led to the unsustainable over-accumulation of wealth and concentration in one place.

The economic depression in the United States triggered a worldwide economic domino effect which some believe to have been primarily caused by halted trade deals and the collapse of the Gold Standard. Even though the US began recovering through Roosevelt's First New Deal, other countries in the world did not see economic relief until after World War II.

## New Deal

Franklin Delano Roosevelt launched New Deal programs in 1933 in response to the Great Depression. They were designed for economic growth, job creation, public works, and civic engagement. They brought the United States out of the depression and laid the foundation for victory in World War II.

Some of the economic stimulation included returning lands to tribal holdings and increasing travel within the United

States, the Glass-Steagall Banking Act and FDIC, and creating Social Security. The Army Corps of Engineers, Bureau of Public Roads, and US Post Office Departments were created, along with many other agencies and programs that still function today. One of the most popular actions for the country repealed Prohibition.

## Cuba

From early settlement to the 1920s, the United States kept a watchful eye on Cuba's rulers, economy, and land ownership, but essentially decided to allow Cuba to control itself and only stepped in when it was necessary to preserve Cuban independence. But by 1929, the United States and US-owned businesses dominated Cuban economy and trade. During the 1940s, Fulgencia Batista, who was known to a supporter of US involvement, became president. He served two terms as president of Cuba, and by the end of his last term in 1959, Cuba was overrun with organized crime.

Fidel Castro and his socialist rebels soon overtook Batista's US-friendly Cuban government and ushered in the Cuban Revolution of 1959. US and Cuban relations disintegrated quickly as the United States learned of Cuba's intent to nationalize control over agriculture and utilities. This was a direct threat to US economic interests in Cuba. From 1961, during the Bay of Pigs invasion, through 1965, there were several US-led attempts at overthrowing the socialist regime which were not successful.

## World War II

It's called "World" War for a reason—it's hard to pinpoint a reason for global fighting when everyone seems to be involved. But in short, fascism in Italy and its invasion of Ethiopia, Japanese militarism and occupation of China, and Germany's Hitler and his Nazi Party, all led to the Second World War The immediate trigger, though, was when Axis forces invaded Poland in 1939, and Britain and France were obligated due to alliance to declare war against Germany. The United States did not become involved until the attack on Pearl Harbor by the Japanese and has been criticized for not getting involved earlier to prevent the Holocaust.

## McCarthyism

McCarthyism references the time of US Senator Joseph McCarthy's time in office, also well known as the Second Red Scare. A staunch anti-Communist conservative, the senator used his role in federal government as a platform to try to eradicate the threat of Communism within its ranks by announcing his list of more than two hundred State Department employees who were allegedly known to be members of the Communist Party.

His term was riddled with arrests, blacklists, and the House Un-American Activities Committee (HUAAC) dealings. HUAAC was most well-known for its focus on the Hollywood movie industry, and in 1947 subpoenaed screenwriters, directors, and other industry professionals to give testimony about alleged membership in, affiliation with, or sympathy to the Communist Party.

Today McCarthyism is a term used to describe regular unsubstantiated attacks of character or politics against political adversaries.

## Truman Doctrine

The Truman Doctrine, developed by President Truman in 1947 and 1948, was foreign policy designed to counter Soviet Cold War expansion. It guaranteed United States assistance to any democratic nations under threat from authoritarian forces, including political, military, and economic help. It was mostly intended as a warning to those the United States felt threatened by, but it was viewed as an effort to help all subjugated peoples, and led to various commitments bigger than anticipated, changing the way the United States was viewed militarily.

## The dark side of Kennedy's legacy

John F. Kennedy was arguably one of our nation's greatest presidents, and after his assassination was viewed on live television, America's tradition of refusal to speak ill of the dead kicked in tenfold, too. He is credited with avoiding World War III with the Cuban Missile Crisis, but he also failed in overthrowing Castro, and the response was to double-down on a dictatorship that imprisoned an island for fifty years. On the flip side, Kennedy is also credited with leading the country into Vietnam, one of the most unpopular wars in history. He had vices unfit for a president—an addiction to methamphetamines because of back pain and an addiction to sex for less socially permissible reasons.

He did great things too, and his favorable legacy is not undeserved. He created the Peace Corps, was a proponent of civil rights, increased welfare and social security benefits, and signed the Equal Pay Act. Kennedy exemplified perhaps the understanding that even great leaders are deeply flawed.

## Brown v Board of Education

This was a pivotal decision of the United States Supreme Court in which the court found that segregation within the state school systems was unconstitutional. This was seen as a huge victory for the civil rights movement; however, the decision was not formed with methods for integration. Although precedent was set in 1954, there were many legislators and state officials, especially in the South, who vehemently opposed the Supreme Court ruling and went so far as to close schools in response.

Texas Attorney General John Ben Shepperd organized for legal obstacles to integration, and more than a hundred officials signed the Southern Manifesto, written in 1956. The Southern Manifesto was written to counter efforts for integration as well as accuse the Supreme Court of "clear abuse of judicial power." However, as we know now, schools soon began integrating, and though there is much work still to be done sixty years later, segregation is now illegal.

## Civil rights movement

The United States Civil Rights Movement was an attempt to end racial segregation and other inequalities while advocating to secure legal recognition of citizenship for African American populations. Garnering attention for its peaceful demonstrations and organized civil disobedience, the movement was successful in influencing a few pieces of legislation between 1955 and 1968. Boycotts, sit-ins, marches, and crusades were organized all over the country to highlight the systematic oppression of the black men, women, and children in the United States.

There were many noteworthy organizers and planners within the movement, one of whom was Bayard Rustin, a leading strategist of the civil rights movement, who was one of the first openly gay, socialist organizers as well. The civil rights movement, by the way, was one of the first large movements with a great deal of inclusivity and intersectionality. Though the focus was on rights for African-Americans and was quite largely Christian-led, it included people of all races and religions, as well as genders and sexualities at the forefront for the first time in US activism history, and paved the way for other social movements.

## Vietnam

The United States became involved in the Vietnam War to prevent Communism from spreading into South Vietnam. This didn't work. America lost, and Vietnam united, remaining Communist to this day. It was an extremely unpopular war. Most Americans didn't see that the United States had anything to gain either way, and sons, brothers, fathers, and husbands were dying in ghastly ways in very high numbers.

The United States lost almost sixty thousand military

personnel, and only about twenty years ago did Vietnam release its estimates—1.1 million fighters in the north, 250,000 in the south, and two million civilians perished. The Vietnam War is also largely credited with the United States' transition from affluence in the 1960s to economic crisis in the 1970s, with consumer confidence and the economy taking a dive.

## Civil Rights Act of 1964

The Civil Rights Act was a turning point in the United States, outlawing discrimination based on race, color, religion, sex, or national origin. It forbade unequal voter registration requirements and segregation, providing employment and public accommodations. The bill was requested by President Kennedy but was signed into law by his successor Lyndon B. Johnson. The bill was passed overwhelmingly, which seems hard to believe in today's divisive political arena, but there were notable exceptions. Arizona Senator Goldwater said, "You can't legislate morality," and Southern state senators also opposed it with unsuccessful 83-day filibusters.

## Apollo

The Apollo space program was the third spaceflight program by the National Aeronautics and Space Administration

(NASA), and it made the first human moon landings from 1969 to 1972. It had been President Kennedy's vision, inspired by the Eisenhower administration's success putting the first Americans in space, to get a man to the moon and then safely landed back on Earth. He set a goal of achieving it by the end of the 1960s. It launched sixteen successful missions and had two failures with one partial failure. The first Apollo failed in a prelaunch test that killed the entire crew. Apollo 11 is the famous flight where Neil Armstrong and Buzz Aldrin landed and walked on the surface. The following five Apollos also landed twelve men on the moon.

# INTERESTING FACTS

1. In 1919 and 1920, the US Justice Department conducted the Palmer Raids, named for the Attorney General of the time, in which suspected leftists were deported from the country. Palmer attempted to remove ten thousand people, and over five hundred were eventually removed. This was part of the larger Red Scare movement.

2. From 1920 to 1933, alcohol sales and production were banned in a period known popularly as Prohibition. In response, the public opened speakeasies. These were illegal bars and got their name because you had to whisper a code word at a locked door to gain entry. New York City alone had more than thirty thousand of these clandestine clubs.

3. Suffragist Alice Paul was instrumental in the passage of the Nineteenth Amendment granting women the right to vote, but she also authored the yet-to-be-ratified Equal Rights Amendment in 1923. Paul was once arrested and sentenced to seven months in jail for protesting at the White House, where she had organized a hunger strike.

4. Charles Lindbergh was a national hero who made the first solo transatlantic flight, but he had a very colorful personal life too. He was a passionate environmental activist, and his firstborn infant son was the kidnap and murder victim of the Crime of the Century. In his youth, he had been thought to be a fascist sympathizer and was vocally antiwar. Later, it was revealed he had fathered seven children by three women (in addition to the six with his wife) in Europe, and two of the women were sisters.

5. Amelia Earhart was the first female aviator to fly across the Atlantic alone, but she disappeared in the Pacific while trying to fly around the globe in 1937. Her death has been shrouded in mystery and is still surrounded by rumor and controversy. Most likely, she crashed at sea, but there are conspiracy theories that are the stuff of thriller novels.

6. In 1938, voice actor Orson Welles did a radio reading of H.G. Wells' *War of the Worlds* that created a mass panic from listeners who thought it was a real news broadcast and that aliens were invading. Makes President Donald Trump's "fake news" claims seem positively real, doesn't it?

7. Albert Einstein was responsible for the Manhattan

Project, which created the first American nuclear bombs. He alerted President Roosevelt that US enemies Japan and Germany would create more advanced nuclear weapons and convinced him to start developing them for the US. However, he wasn't a part of the project—he couldn't get security clearance! He was a little too leftist for the government's comfort.

8. Internment camps were established during World War II housing 115,000 Japanese Americans because Americans feared they would aid the enemy in the war. The forced removal of US citizens is today known to be one of the worst civil rights violations in United States history.

9. Franklin Delano Roosevelt is one of the country's most memorable presidents for a myriad of reasons. The only president to be elected four times, he spent much of his adult life, including the presidency, in a wheelchair. He created the New Deal and saw the US through World War II, and his wife Eleanor was one of the most adored First Ladies of all time.

10. The first McDonald's opened in 1937 in Monrovia, California, but it was very different from what we know today, with mainly hot dogs, all you can drink orange juice, and barbecue, in a carhop drive-in setting.

It's now the largest restaurant company in the world.

11. The Hindenburg was a German passenger airship that caught fire in 1937, killing more than a third on board and a worker on the ground. If you're questioning what an airship is, there's good reason. It's just a hot air balloon, but now we use them for advertising and aerial surveys among other small novelty reasons. The Hindenburg was the end of the short-lived era in which these large hot air balloons were used for mass travel.

12. Pearl Harbor was the 1941 Japanese attack on the United States that marked the US entrance into World War II, hitting a Hawaiian naval base, and killing more than 2,400 American military. Truman forced Japan's surrender by attacking Hiroshima and Nagasaki with atom bombs, killing over a hundred thousand civilians and injuring twice as many, causing some illnesses due to radiation that still exist there today.

13. In Nuremberg, Germany, in 1945 and 1946, the United States and other Allied countries presided over hearings for 22 Nazi war criminals. Twelve were sentenced to hanging. The Nuremberg principles were then established by the United Nations to set a guideline for what constituted a war crime.

14. In 1947, Jackie Robinson broke "the color line" by

becoming the first African American player in Major League Baseball. He played for the Brooklyn Dodgers when the MLB had been segregated for half a century.

15. In 1947, the US Air Force crashed a weather balloon near Roswell, New Mexico. *So they say.* One of America's favorite conspiracy theories is that it was a UFO, aliens were captured by the military, and there has been a massive cover-up ever since. I'm still upset about Lindbergh and Roosevelt, so I don't know what to believe.

16. The Korean War began in 1950 when North Korea invaded South Korea, which was supported by the United States. The US was involved (in part) because it didn't want Communism to spread. There were more than sixty thousand deaths and missing in action US personnel, and the US still maintains a heavy peacekeeping military presence.

17. The polio vaccine was invented in 1953 by virologist Jonas Salk, and Roosevelt helped make it happen after being stricken with the disease himself, thus bringing attention to it. While polio was serious and has nearly been eradicated, it wasn't actually as deadly as history paints it. After World War II, Americans only feared nuclear war more than polio, yet childhood accidents

killed ten times as many children and cancer had a three to one death rate.

18. Disneyland opened in 1955, and what is now one of America's childhood treasures nearly never came to pass, as the opening was an utter disaster. Temperatures reached 100 degrees, asphalt melted, Mark Twain's riverboat capsized, not all rides were ready, counterfeit tickets doubled the guest list, there was a critical food shortage, and there was a seven-mile backup on the Santa Ana Freeway. It's still known as "Black Sunday."

19. Emmett Till's life is a sad and tragic story that must be told in American history to prevent it from happening again. In 1955, a fourteen-year-old African American child was lynched because a white woman accused him of sexual assault, which she later admitted was not true. His killers were acquitted, but the tragedy fueled the civil rights movement.

20. John F. Kennedy, Jr., one of the most popular presidents in American history, was assassinated on November 22, 1963, and his murder has no shortage of conspiracy theories. The only thing we know for sure is that a Roswell alien probably isn't responsible, but Lee Harvey Oswald, who was convicted, is up for debate—

especially after recently released FBI files that make director Hoover seem very eager to convince the public.

# TEST YOURSELF

1.  What exactly was the Hindenburg?

    A)  The first space mission

    B)  A wartime submarine

    C)  A passenger airship

2.  Who gave us the Peace Corps?

    A)  Franklin Delano Roosevelt

    B)  John F. Kennedy, Jr.

    C)  Jackie Robinson

3.  In what year did women get the right to vote?

    A)  1920

    B)  1919

    C)  1878

4.  Hiroshima was retaliation for what event?

    A)  Nagasaki

    B)  The Holocaust

    C)  Pearl Harbor

5.  Who was the first man on the moon?

    A)  Paul Alice

    B)  Neil Armstrong

    C)  Orson Welles

## ANSWERS

1. C
2. B
3. A
4. C
5. B

# CHAPTER FIVE

# 1964 – NOW
# CIVIL RIGHTS TO "OH MY GOD, WHAT HAVE WE DONE?"

The Civil Rights Movement is when the United States started to get into a groove. Hey, we're going to right these wrongs slowly but surely, and somehow, we're going to make space for everyone under the equality umbrella. That hasn't come without its setbacks and mistakes, but the last fifty-odd years have shown much progress in making the effort. To some people, the last few years, or perhaps months, feels like it's going in the wrong direction, but the jury is still out, so we'll keep the negativity to ourselves and focus on rainbows. And there are a lot of rainbows in this chapter!

## Stonewall Riots

As recently as the 1960s and 1970s, LGBT folks in the United States were legally prohibited from engaging in their lifestyles and few establishments permitted them to openly frequent and meet other people. Of those that did, bars were the most commonly encountered venues but were also subject to frequent police raids that bordered on and sometimes crossed well over to harassment.

Greenwich Village was a tolerant, liberal-leaning neighborhood in New York City, and on June 28, 1969, when police raided and harangued gay patrons at the Stonewall Inn, patrons and townspeople fought back, first on the streets outside the bar and then as an organized community effort to provide a safe haven for LGBT to live publicly. The efforts are credited with ushering in the modern era of the LGBT tolerance and rights movements, and the day is celebrated yearly with gay pride parades across the country.

## Roe v Wade

In case you hadn't heard about this completely uncontroversial and boring little Supreme Court ruling, in 1973, abortion was made legal in the United States. A pregnant woman had sued to obtain an abortion in Texas, where it was prohibited except to save a woman's life. The case went all the way to the Supreme Court, along with another lesser known case, Doe v. Bolton, and together the cases restricted states' rights to limit access to abortion procedures and prevented them from prosecuting women who sought them.

The Court ruled abortion was covered as a matter of privacy rights and that states could not interfere. Debates of this highly divisive ruling continue, and access gets closer and closer to pre-1973 restrictions all the time. However, legally, abortion access is still protected in the United States under Roe v. Wade and Doe v. Bolton.

## Watergate

Arguably the largest modern political scandal involving abuses of power occurred during President Richard Nixon's administration and was uncovered in June 1972, starting with a break-in by five burglars at the Democratic National Committee headquarters in the Watergate Office Complex in Washington, D.C. Congress investigated the incident while Nixon's administration attempted to cover it up and resisted the investigation.

A series of other illegal and unethical tactics undertaken by members of the administration were also uncovered, such as bugging offices of opponents and ordering FBI, CIA, and IRS investigation of members of activist groups and political figures. The Congressional findings created a constitutional crisis that led to President Nixon's unprecedented resignation on August 9, 1974, in the face of certain impeachment. He was pardoned a month later by successor Gerald Ford.

## Challenger Disaster

In one of the first national disasters to be widely televised and immediately viewed, the NASA Space Shuttle Challenger and its mission orbiter blew up 73 seconds after launch on January 28, 1986. All seven crew members—five astronauts, including Krista McAuliffe, the first teacher sent to space, and two others—were killed instantly. The launch occurred under unusually cold conditions, causing a piece to fail and leading to the explosion over the Atlantic Ocean.

NASA space operations were suspended for 32 months while a thorough investigation was ordered, finding that the 1977 designs for the booster rockets contained a weakness in the failed piece that had been reported and ignored. The case is often used a as a case study for workplace ethics and safety. An estimated seventeen percent of the US watched the launch live, and within an hour, roughly 85 percent had witnessed the footage. Many of the viewers were schoolchildren.

## Iran-Contra Affair

President Ronald Reagan found his plans for foreign influence legally impeded by Congress during the second term of his Presidency in what might be one of the most fascinating but hard to keep up with scandals in politics to date. In an attempt to both free US hostages by Islamic Revolution and Iranian forces in Lebanon, Reagan and his administration organized a hidden deal that encompassed Iran, Israel, and, through sleight of hand, Nicaragua.

The US sold arms and munitions to a sympathetic Iranian group, using Israel as the intermediary. The money from the sales was used to illegally fund the Nicaraguan right-wing Contras, who were, like several other Central American nations, toppling progressive rights and land reform elected governments. The US had been previously supporting these efforts, classifying Central America's governments as leftist/Communist in nature.

In exchange for the arms, on the other side of the ocean, the Iranians were supposed to negotiate the freeing of the hostages. The story broke to national humiliation in November 1986. Several high-ranking officials were eventually implicated in the scandal and prepared to face charges; however, the majority of the charges were eventually dropped and the players pardoned during H.W. Bush's administration.

## Gulf War

In the largest international coalition since World War II, a seven-month war was fought in the Persian Gulf and Iraq from August 1990 through February 1991. The war was fought over the aggressive act by Iraq in the invasion and annexation of Kuwait, a move that was strongly condemned by the UN Security council and that led to economic sanctions. US President H. W. Bush sent troops to Saudi Arabia, encouraging other nations to join. All told, 35 nations participated in the effort to free Kuwait.

The war became one of the first military operations to be widely televised, with CNN news reporters on the war's front lines for the first time in history. The ground offensive was geographically limited and relatively quick. A ceasefire was declared after Iraq's forces were ousted from Kuwait. The two major operations of the war were known respectively as "Operation Desert Shield" and "Operation Desert Storm."

## Oklahoma City bombing

In the single largest incident to date of domestic terrorism, Timothy McVeigh, Terry Nichols, and some accomplices bombed the Alfred P. Murrah Building in downtown Oklahoma City on April 19, 1995. Timed to coincide with the fatal Waco Texas shootout years earlier, the bomb blasts killed 168 people, injured more than 680 others, and damaged or destroyed 324 other buildings within a sixteen-block radius.

McVeigh was a Gulf War vet who was highly critical of the US government, hence the bombings and their timing. In direct response to the attack, the United States Congress in 1996 passed legislation that increased security around federal buildings and that also changed the standards for the death penalty and habeas corpus. McVeigh was executed in 1997, and Nichols was sentenced to life in prison. The Oklahoma City National Memorial was erected on the site in 2000, and annual remembrances are held each year at the timing of the bombing.

## Barack Obama

Coming into office in 2009, in the midst of the largest world economic recession since the Great Depression, 44th President Barack Obama would have been noteworthy as a president if all he had done was to prevent further economic downturn in the US. However, history will remember him more as the first African-American US President and for his domestic and international policies. A previous civil rights attorney and groundbreaking constitutional law professor, Obama served as Illinois State Senator prior to his 2008 Presidential nomination.

Shortly into his presidency, he became the third US President to be awarded the Nobel Peace Prize. He had a very controversial two-term presidency, though many felt much of the criticism was undeserved, and he left office with a favorable approval rating. His wife was also one of the most popular First Ladies in history, though that was somewhat controversial as well.

## Reagan Presidency

The election and service of the fortieth US President, Ronald Wilson Reagan, from 1981-1988, is historically seen as a shift towards a conservative mindset for policy, after US social and economic policy had been trending progressive for some time. An actor and union leader prior to his election as California governor, Reagan became the spokesperson for conservatism in the United States after working to unearth Communist influence in the Screen Actors Guild while serving as their president and a hard stance towards student protestors as governor of California. He unsuccessfully ran for the US Presidential ticket twice before winning both the ticket and the race in 1980 against incumbent Jimmy Carter. He was the first President since the 1950s to serve two terms.

He was remembered in his presidency for the "trickle-down" economic policies called Reaganomics, which purported that tax cuts lead to sustained economic growth. Under his presidency, investment in domestic government spending was cut, while military influence was increased. He easily won a second term in a landslide election, with his second term being marked by the impending end of the Cold War, military engagements in Central America, the Iran-Contra Affair, and an escalating arms race which eventually led to the INF treaty reducing nuclear stockpiles. The Berlin Wall and Soviet Union both fell shortly after his presidency. He left office with a mixed legacy but one of the highest approval ratings of any modern US president. He died of Alzheimer's Disease in 1994 and survived an assassination attempt during his presidency.

## Morris Worm

Nicknamed the "Great Worm," a literary reference to JRR Tolkien's dragons, the Morris Worm was one of the first extremely dangerous and costly computer data worm programs in the early days of internet popularity. It also resulted in the first felony conviction of creators of such programs. Launched by Cornell graduate student Robert Tappan Morris on November 2, 1988, from computer systems at the Massachusetts Institute of Technology, the worm infected an estimated ten percent of all sixty thousand Unix machines operating at the time on the internet. It entered via the email system and weak passwords, and was self-replicating, rendering machines increasingly slow to the point of non-functionality. Clean-up was slow and costly, and the internet was shut down for several days for the necessary repairs to be made.

Although Morris claimed the program was meant to be investigative in nature, not destructive, he was fined and sentenced to three years' probation plus community service. DARPA (Defense Advanced Research Projects Agency, an arm of the US Department of Defense) responded to the incident by establishing a coordinated response center to future cyber-attacks on critical systems.

## Hurricane Katrina

The year 2005 was extremely active for hurricanes, and one of the deadliest on record, Hurricane Katrina, became the eleventh named storm of the season and the eleventh to develop into a hurricane when she hit the coasts of Florida, Mississippi, and Louisiana in August. The destruction left in her wake made her one of the five deadliest storms on record, and the costliest to date. 1,245 deaths were directly attributed to Katrina, and over 108 billion dollars in damages were incurred and reimbursed. The most damaging effects were not the winds but the incredible storm surge, which reached up to twelve miles or more inland and overtook fifty levee systems in New Orleans, where most of the deaths occurred.

The devastation caused by the storm was so great that several formal investigations were made into the systemic infrastructure and human failures. US agencies were also both lauded and heavily criticized, depending on the agency in question. President George W. Bush's leadership received the heaviest criticism. Most heavily hit were the poorest sectors and people of color.

## War in Afghanistan

When Al Qaeda leader Osama bin Laden claimed responsibility for the 9/11/2001 terrorist attacks, President George W. Bush launched Operation Enduring Freedom against Afghanistan. His aim was to remove the Taliban from power, thus removing a safe haven for Al Qaeda to operate and destroying the terrorist group. All Northern Alliance and NATO members eventually joined the fight, and the Afghanistan War has become the single longest conflict in US history.

Although President Obama was able to eliminate bin Laden and draft an exit strategy for removal of all but contingency ground forces, as of May 2017 there were still thirteen thousand ground troops in the country with no immediate plans for further withdrawal. The war has exacted a very heavy economic, emotional, and casualty toll on the forces involved, with over 4,000 ISAF military deaths, 31,000 civilian casualties, and more than 15,000 Afghani military losses. The current provisionary government, on its own after UN withdrawal, is considered shaky at best.

## Rise in technology use

If Alexander Graham Bell had been told his crazy little invention of the telephone would one day end up wireless and sized to the palm of a hand, he'd have thought you were crazy. Moreover, if you'd have told him all that data and so much more would fly through tiny wires into electronic boxes called computers, he'd have laughed you right out of his lab, and you would have completely changed the course of history because he'd have never invented the thing. So, thank goodness you kept that one to yourself.

I still don't know who invented the internet, I just know it wasn't Al Gore, and another Al G. is kind of its great-great-grandfather. When I was a young'un, we didn't have cell phones, and telephones were hooked to walls with curled cords. I was the only kid on the block with a computer, and I used it to play Wheel of Fortune in black and green pixels when my dad wasn't doing boring accounting stuff.

Now, those wall beasts are almost as antique as the big blocks of computer that took up entire desks. Every member of the family has a cell phone by age ten (and that age appears to be decreasing), and if each member doesn't have a laptop and a tablet too, we feel deprived. Other electronics such as headsets, headphones, and gaming devices, GPS and MP3 players will vary depending on the user, but the first three appear to be as necessary as oxygen and water.

To demonstrate just how quickly we've become dependent on these devices, the Pew Research Center says in 2009, 31 percent of US adults owned a cell phone; in 2012, ninety percent of them did, and 55 percent of them used it to connect to the internet. The dependence has gone global faster than most trends – the US and other developed countries has had some transition difficulty retrofitting existing infrastructure to digital technology, but developing countries shifted right to it, lacking the heavy landline infrastructure.

## Tea Party protests

The Tea Party movement was a series of loosely-organized protests that occurred mostly between 2007 and 2011, with the intent of creating discontent over what protesters saw as the overreach of big government. Named in honor of the Boston Tea Party protesters prior to the Revolutionary War, many protestors used the acronym "TEA" to stand for

"Taxed Enough Already." Protesters held events to raise campaign funds for Libertarian and future alt-right candidates, to protest economic stimulus, to protest Tax Day, to coincide with major national holidays, to protest health care reform, and later, to generally protest all of President Barack Obama's policies.

The group started to fade into the background of other emerging alt-right movements starting around 2011. During the height of the movement, the Tea Party movement received a lot of press coverage and was considered a strong influential force in the elections for House and Senate that returned full control to Conservatives. There is evidence that the movement was not as grassroots as the organizers claimed, but rather, was an action funded by high-level conservative investors.

## The launch of Facebook

As the internet became more and more of a phenomenon, uses and ideas evolved. Several social media platforms like MySpace and chat forums began creating buzz, and in 2004, Mark Zuckerberg and some Harvard roommates created Facebook. Named after university directories, also called "face books," the website allowed users at Harvard, and later the public, to connect with each other in a social media platform whose importance and impact was just emerging and being understood. By June 2017, the platform had over two billion users, just over one-fifth of the world's population.

Not without controversy, Facebook makes its money off advertising algorithms and highly specialized ad campaigns. Its influence has been linked to mental health issues, activist planning, influencing of political elections, and hundreds of other applications. As with most technologies, its policies, platform, and functionality have evolved to address user needs, concerns, and demands.

# INTERESTING FACTS

1.  Congress adopted the 25th Amendment in 1965, and the states ratified it in 1967. A favorite obsession of forlorn political junkies whose presidential pick loses the election, it determines the order of succession if the President is assassinated or unfit to serve. A fun game is to see who holds each position and determine if the President happened to call a Cabinet meeting on a boat that springs a leak with no life rafts, how many ranking members need to be on the boat and who needs to stay on shore. Not that I've played this game, I swear. This amendment was discussed previously but developed and passed shortly after the assassination of Kennedy because of concerns with the health of those in succession after him.

2.  Mildred and Richard Loving married in the 1960s, but the state of Virginia sentenced them to a year in prison under the Racial Integrity Act. Why? Because Mildred was black, and Richard was white. Their case went to the Supreme Court in 1967, and Loving v. VA overturned the Act legalizing interracial marriage for all states. They went to have a happy life together and had three children—almost like a normal healthy

marriage has nothing to do with color!

3. In the words of Scott McKenzie, in the summer of 1967, a hundred thousand people who identified with the hippie peace movement descended upon the San Francisco Haight-Ashbury neighborhood to "wear a flower in [their] hair" and discuss poetry, art, music, politics, spirituality, and philosophy. It was the largest gathering of what became known as the Summer of Love and remained influential for decades to come.

4. The first show to measure its impact on children's learning, Sesame Street has been a wildly successful experiment in combining the expertise of producers, writers, educators, and researchers. By 1996, it was estimated that 95 percent of US preschool children had watched the long-running PBS show—over 77 million viewers in the US and an additional fifty million in 140 other countries. The show has won more Emmy and Grammy awards than any other children's show in history.

5. US politician, educator, and writer Shirley Chisholm became the first black woman elected to Congress in 1968. She represented the twelfth district of New York for seven terms, from 1969 until 1983. In 1973, she set another precedent as the first woman presidential

candidate for a major party. President Obama posthumously awarded her the Presidential Medal of Freedom in 2015.

6. The complex relationship that rival organizations can create, and their interdependence, can be seen perfectly in the forty-year on-again, off-again friendship and competition between tech giants Microsoft and Apple. Although Microsoft is, by design, a software creator, and Apple a creator of hardware devices, the two companies have created a synergy that led much of the Information Age's most versatile and useful technology—especially when they set gloves aside and worked together to get Microsoft's programs onto Apple machines and vice-versa.

7. The largest single deliberate act that resulted in loss of US civilian life prior to 9/11 was the Jonestown massacre of November 1978, where 909 people died from drinking poison under duress, and nine others were murdered, all under orders. The mastermind of the event, charismatic cult leader Jim Jones, had created a US socialist colony in the capital city Georgetown of the South American country of Guyana.

8. The worst commercial nuclear incident in US history

occurred on March 28, 1979, in a nuclear power plant located in the middle of the Susquehanna River, just outside of Harrisburg, PA. You may have heard of it as the Three Mile Island nuclear disaster. A series of cooling system failures in Reactor 2 caused a partial meltdown and release of radioactive material. Follow-up studies indicated no long-term measurable side effects, although the incident triggered public safety concerns and a downturn in new plant construction.

9. The Iran hostage crisis was the longest hostage standoff in recorded history. Iranian students overtook the US embassy and took 52 US diplomats and citizens hostage on November 4, 1979. They were released 444 days later.

10. The shift of popular music from being a form that is listened to, to one that is watched, was Viacom Media Network's launch of MTV Music Television on August 1, 1981. The new visual format launched completely new musical artforms, revolutionizing the already lucrative music industry. The station is found in approximately ninety million US households today, but you know, in my day, MTV actually played music.

11. The entrance of women into the highest court of the land happened under Ronald Reagan's administration,

when, in 1981, he appointed Justice Sandra Day O'Connor as the first US Supreme Court judge. She served to retirement in 2005.

12. In the days before organizing via widespread internet and social media, the fundraising and publicity campaign "Hands Across America" briefly united the country in 1986. From coast to coast, in the lower 48 states, 6.5 million people held hands for fifteen minutes, promoting unity and poverty awareness.

13. Pan Am Flight 103 was one leg of a regularly scheduled route from Frankfurt to Detroit. On December 21, 1988, terrorists detonated a bomb on board over Lockerbie, Scotland, killing 243 passengers, sixteen crew, and eleven people on the ground. The incident was linked to Gaddafi's Libyan regime.

14. One of the closest Presidential elections of modern US history was the 2000 race between former vice president Al Gore and Texas governor George W. Bush. The race came down to deciding who won the state of Florida, and the ballots were so close that a recount was ordered. The US Supreme Court was called upon to decide the election. County records swayed the election for Bush; had the popular vote

been counted, Gore would have won.

15. Although mass shootings and even school shootings had occurred previously, the modern phenomenon of deadly mass school shootings was realized with Eric Harris and Dylan Klebold's 1999 attacks on Columbine High School in Colorado. Twelve students and one teacher died, and 24 more were injured. The case has been widely analyzed for clues into the psyches of would-be mass murderers in an effort to prevent what is seen as a growing epidemic in US culture.

16. In 2000, the population of New Orleans was close to 500,000. 2005's Hurricane Katrina devastated eighty percent of the city's buildings, resulting in a net population migration loss by 2006 of over fifty percent. The population rose steadily with recovery and rebuilding efforts, and in 2015, the city was back up to 390,000 residents.

17. One of the most award-winning and critically acclaimed popular music performers of all time, Michael Jackson's 1983 Thriller album, remains the highest selling album of all time. Even after his 2009 death Jackson continues to set the record for the highest earning dead celebrity, his estate earning 825

million dollars in 2016 alone.

18. The Supreme Court decided in 2015 that states' efforts to deny marriage certificates to same-sex couples was a violation of the Fourteenth Amendment. The practice of same-sex marriage was legalized at the federal level with that ruling, and rainbows beamed all over the country.

19. The Americans with Disabilities Act of 1990 afforded protections to Americans living with physical or mental disabilities. The ADA cited non-discrimination and provided that employers and public spaces would be required to provide accommodations for disabled workers and users.

20. Between 1958 and 1962, under growing US-Cuba tensions, the US enacted an almost complete embargo on all trade between the US and the Communist Cuba. In 2015, President Obama opened the door for missionary and educational visits and lifted many trade restrictions, thus effectively ending the decades-long embargo.

# TEST YOURSELF

1.  Who was the first woman to serve on the United States Supreme Court?

    A) Shirley Chisholm
    B) Sandra Day O'Connor
    C) Mildred Loving

2.  In what city was the Stonewall Inn located?

    A) New York City
    B) San Francisco
    C) New Orleans

3.  Which President successfully ordered the death of Osama bin Laden?

    A) Donald Trump
    B) George W. Bush
    C) Barack Obama

4.  Who decided the vote in the 2000 election?

    A) The United States Supreme Court
    B) Shirley Chisholm
    C) Dade County, Florida

5. What album is the biggest selling of all time?

   A) Like A Virgin
   B) Thriller
   C) Space Oddity

## ANSWERS

1. B
2. A
3. C
4. A
5. B

# CHAPTER SIX

# MORE PIVOTAL MOMENTS IN UNITED STATES HISTORY

The United States of America is young, but if you haven't noticed, we like drama around here, and a lot has happened. We hold a grudge too. Chris Columbus has still not apologized for what he did more than five hundred years ago, and I'm waiting. So just in case you missed some of the gossip, here are a few more highlights to chat about around the office water cooler. You didn't hear any of this from me, but…

## Assassination of Abraham Lincoln

Abraham Lincoln was the 16th US President and was the first US President to be assassinated. On April 14th, 1865, while attending the play "Our American Cousin" in Ford's Theater in Washington, D.C., he was shot in the head by the famous actor, John Wilkes Booth. He died from his injuries the following morning, at 7:22 am. His assassination precipitated a months-long period of national mourning. Booth's motivation was an attempted revival of Confederate causes and interests.

Lincoln is consistently ranked as one of the United States' greatest presidents. He was succeeded by his vice-president, Andrew Johnson.

## Louisiana Purchase

The third US president, Thomas Jefferson, negotiated the purchase of territory that would become part of fifteen US states, stretching in a swath from New Orleans, Louisiana, to the Canadian border of Alberta. The land was previously under the jurisdiction of France, and the US government negotiated the purchase with Emperor Napoleon in 1803. The purchase greatly expanded the territory to cover almost all land of North America between Canada and Mexico, and East of the Rocky Mountain Continental Divide.

## Manhattan Project

The Manhattan Project was a four-year initiative for the development, testing, and creation of the world's first atomic weapons. The project leaders were a US-led coalition that included support from the United Kingdom and Canada, with over 130,000 people involved at more than 30 sites across the three countries. Major General Leslie Groves of the US Army Corps of Engineers was the project's overall director, while physicist Robert Oppenheimer was responsible for the actual creation of bombs. The US used the first atomic weapon in battle with Japan, a highly controversial decision that has been credited with bringing the Pacific Theater conflict of World War II to its end. The creation of nuclear weapons forever changed the context of warfare.

## Vietnam War

The Vietnam War, also known as "The Second Indochina War," was a war fought in French Indochina between northern and southern factions of the country of Vietnam, in Vietnam, Cambodia, and Laos, in an attempt to unify the two halves of the nation of Vietnam. The start and end dates were from November 1, 1955, to the Fall of Saigon, April 30, 1975. The US became involved slowly in the 1950s, supporting South Vietnam (with aid from Australia and South Korea), against China, Soviet, and Communist ally-supported North Vietnam. US involvement was heightened over the following two decades and was justified at the time as part of the "containment policy" for preventing the expansion of Communist influence.

Thus, the Vietnam War is considered a part of Cold War engagement. The war had a very high death toll on all sides and sparked a national protest movement—and great social division—in the US. Some 58,220 US service members died in the conflict, and a further 1,626 remain missing in action. The US officially left the war in August of 1973. The war marked the last time a US draft was issued for combat.

## Death of Osama bin Laden

Osama Bin Laden was the founder and head of the terrorist group Al-Qaeda, based in the Middle East. He took credit as the mastermind of the September 11, 2001, attacks in the United States. The US invaded Afghanistan shortly after the attacks in an initiative to capture and destroy Al-Qaeda leaders and installations. The action spread to Pakistan, where Al-Qaeda had bases and headquarters. On May 2, 2011, US Navy Seals and Naval Special Warfare Development group personnel carried out "Operation Neptune Spear," which killed Bin Laden in his compound in Abbottabad, Pakistan. This ended a 10-year search for Bin Laden and his operatives.

The raid was lauded by 90 percent of the US, the United Nations, NATO, and the European Union, but was condemned by many others, including the Pakistani populace. Tensions remain high in the region, and the US is still involved in a conflict in the region (as of 2017) despite having achieved this primary objective.

## Assassination of John F. Kennedy

John F. Kennedy was the 35th US President. He was assassinated in Dealey Plaza in Dallas, Texas, on November 22, 1963, while riding in a motorcade with his wife, Jacqueline, and Texas Governor John Connally and his wife, Nellie. The shooter was identified as Lee Harvey Oswald, a former US Marine.

A Senate committee known as the Warren Commission conducted a 10-month investigation into the assassination, identified Oswald as the lone gunman, and concluded that he acted alone. Before going to trial, Oswald was himself shot on national television by Jack Ruby, who also apparently acted alone. A 1979 investigative committee, the HCSA, challenged the Warren Report with the assertion that there was evidence for a conspiracy in Kennedy's death.

To this day, the matter has not been conclusively settled. Kennedy's death marked a national period of deep mourning and is credited with having changed the nature of US public trust in the government. Lyndon Johnson became President upon Kennedy's death.

## American Revolution

The United States War of Independence lasted from 1775 to 1783 and was the result of tensions between the thirteen

North American colonies and the British. Patriots cried for "no taxation without representation," and the British only insisted on more, leading to the Boston Tea Party tax protests. The first shot rang out on April 19, 1775, and is called the "shot heard round the world."

Another fun fact—the Continental Congress (meaning the colonists) couldn't afford a navy, so they hired pirates to attack ships from Britain. The booty was to be split with the United States. No word if that end of the bargain was kept, but that's some great American entrepreneurial spirit!

## Civil War

Tensions were rising to an explosion point in the South over slavery versus abolition, and the South decided to secede from the Union. The Union and the Confederacy declared war on one another and suddenly the United States of America found itself fighting amongst one another in its first, and thankfully only, civil war. It's one of the longest lasting battles in the country, lasting over four years, and it ended with up to one million dead, lasting from 1861 to 1865. In the end, the Union won and slavery was abolished, with ramifications of war eventually leading to the collapse of the southern states. Territories were destroyed, soldiers were dead, and the economy was completely in shambles—with their free labor gone so no manner to rebuild. In turn, freed slaves began the process of earning their citizenship and rights.

## September 11, 2001

9/11 is known as the day modern American lost its innocence. Everyone over the age of 21 can likely tell you where they were when this occurred, and some can't do it without tears, even if they didn't lose a loved one. On this day, two planes were crashed into fields, and both towers of the World Trade Center were attacked also using two commercial airliners—with thousands inside. On what everyone remembers as a perfect fall morning, one of the largest terrorist attacks on American soil occurred before our eyes on live television.

Almost 3,000 people died, and 6,000 more were injured. Al-Qaeda took credit for it. The seemingly indestructible towers fell on live television with people still trapped inside, and today in their place stands a memorial and museum, with two reflecting pools placed exactly where the towers were. Since the attack, the United States has been in constant conflict to bring the responsible parties to justice. Though the leader of Al-Qaeda, Osama bin Laden, was killed, his weakened organization still exists.

## Apollo 11

Apollo 11 landed the first people on the moon. Neil Armstrong was commander, and his pilot Buzz Aldrin became the next to do so six hours later. The mission went on for eight days, and the men brought back over thirty pounds of lunar material. Like all good things in America, there's a conspiracy theory about it because no one wants to believe it's real, and this one comes with its fair share. Many people believe the landing was done on a sound stage because the Russians were getting too close to a moon landing, and the United States had to get there first. There have been elaborate reenactments, and depending on who you believe, it is either highly probable or definitely impossible it was faked.

## Election Day 2016

On Election Day 2016, the majority of America found itself in surprise. Reality television star and billionaire Donald Trump won the presidency in what appeared to be a landslide. One problem though—all polling had indicated that his opponent, first female Democrat presidential candidate Hillary Clinton, would be the one winning by a landslide. While the polling errors are a whole other debate, and the science behind this is now being reanalyzed like never before, another issue split the country. He had run a bad campaign with poor messaging, and had in fact made a platform out of bullying, according to some.

People turned on one another for their voting choices, but the interesting problem is that Trump didn't win because the people voted for him. To date, there is an investigation regarding voting fraud, but that's still open and too big to speculate. What is more interesting is that he won, and the people DIDN'T vote for him. Hillary Clinton won the popular vote by an impressive margin, yet Trump just barely edged out in key states so that he won the Electoral College.

Many have argued for years that the Electoral College was obsolete and this could happen, while others knew it was obsolete but didn't see this coming and didn't think it was so important. The rest of the voters are just learning what in the world an Electoral College is and how all those smart professors could have messed this up.

## Lewis & Clark

The Lewis & Clark expedition is one of the most well-known and frankly romanticized stories in American history. Both Americans, they were sent by Jefferson to explore the area of the Louisiana Purchase. This was the first American expedition, and they had the tasks of setting

132

up trade areas, researching flora and fauna, and getting a general feel for all the areas. Along the way, there were various encounters with Native American tribes, including various "almost-fights" and plenty of disputes.

Lewis and Clark managed to make it out unscathed and had the famous Sacagawea join them. She could speak the language of the Shoshone, which they needed along the journey. She proved invaluable to them in exploring the territories and mapping the area for the United States.

## Indian Removal Act

In 1830, President Andrew Jackson signed into law the Indian Removal Act. This allowed him to remove Native Americans from their land and place them into unsettled territories west of the Mississippi River. However, this was only legal if it was done by exchanging lands. They got around this by creating Indian reservations and forcing tribes into these new locations. Later in the winter, the government went on to remove the Cherokee, which led to another infamous tragedy, the Trail of Tears. This caused the deaths of another four thousand Cherokee natives. While there are a few tribes that left their lands without a fight, many of them resisted and were violently forced out, even causing war.

## Mexican-American War

From 1846 to 1848, the United States and Mexico warred amongst neighbors. Most commonly known as the Mexican-American war, it's also called the American Intervention in Mexico. At the time, Mexico considered Texas to be in their territory, as they had assisted in the Texas revolution just a decade earlier in 1836. Mexico hadn't prepared for war and had been weakened by Native American attacks in their territories as well. During the war, it was expected that the people of Texas would side with Mexico, but prior to the war, the United States had declared Texas to be a part of its territory, and the people had to pick sides. As it turns out, Texans mostly revolted against Mexico, and this greatly contributed to Mexico's loss in the war and of their territory.

## The Great Depression

The Great Depression began in 1929 with Black Tuesday, the day the stock market crashed, losing twelve points in one day after having slowly but continuously dropped for about six weeks. Within three years, unemployment had risen to 25 percent and worldwide gross domestic product fallen by 15 percent. To this day, it's the largest and most widespread economic depression the United States has ever faced. For comparison, during the Great Recession of 2008-

2009, the GDP fell less than 1 percent.

The numbers sound awful, but what it looked like in reality was even bleaker. There was no work to be had anywhere, with no money to purchase necessities, and then necessities weren't to be found as stores could no longer stock. Construction projects halted whether they were in the beginning stages or near the end, and farmers lost everything as they began to make only a fraction of the value of their produce. Food supplies dwindled, and hunger increased. With nothing coming in, nothing could go out either. Roosevelt's New Deal policies are credited with the turnaround, though critics say they weren't aggressive enough to help the economy fully recover.

The depression continued into World War II, and ironically while wars often destroy economies, in this case it may have ended the economic crisis when men were sent to war and women replaced them in the workforce. Once men returned from the war, often both partners stayed in the workforce, providing two incomes for households and greater work output for the country.

# INTERESTING FACTS

1. The most famous character anecdote of George Washington was his "cherry tree story," in which Washington's integrity was exemplified. The story goes that young George received a new hatchet and chopped down his father's cherry tree. When confronted, he said "I cannot tell a lie!" and he confessed. His father praised his honesty, but ironically, the story is a myth.

2. Jesse James was an American outlaw who in the late nineteenth century who was known for being the American Robin Hood, stealing from rich corporations to give to poor farmers. Like all great American legends, it's probably false.

3. Unlike most of the wars in modern history, the Cold War referred to growing animosity but not actual war between former World War allies from 1947 to the early 90s. A lot of interesting facts come out of this strange time, but just one is that Congress added "under God" to the Pledge of Allegiance in this period to symbolize resistance to Communists.

4. Prior to the 1961 construction of the Berlin Wall

separating Soviet bloc country East Germany from economically progressive West Germany, over 3.5 million East Germans seeking a better life defected from East Germany into Western Europe. The wall effectively stopped such migrations for 28 years.

5. Famous plane hijacker DB Cooper probably borrowed his name from a Belgian comic book series depicting the derring-do of a Royal Canadian Air Force test pilot Dan Cooper. A massive decades-long search involving over 1000 military personnel and equipment turned up no trace of Cooper after he parachuted from a plane over Washington State in 1971.

6. Prior to their scandalous downfall and removal from televangelist activities, Jim and Tammy Faye Bakker were receiving an estimated $1 million per week in donations for fraudulent religious purposes.

7. Lana Turner was an American film actress, often credited with being one of the first women in film to portray the inner turmoil of their private lives in the roles they cast. She married eight times to seven different men, openly battled depression and mental illness, and fought a scandal when her fourteen-year-old killed a former lover of Lana's who was threatening the family.

8. In the early days of US colonialism, the six Iroquois Nations formed the "Confederacy" and remained loyal to each other. A split in the Confederacy came during the US War for Independence. The Tuscarora and Oneida sided with US colonists, and the Mohawk, Seneca, Onondaga, and Cayuga sided with the British, with whom they had stronger trading ties. The Mohawk were especially affected by this decision, and retaliations against them by colonists forced the relocation of most of their tribal members to Canada.

9. During the decade preceding the Civil War, Lawrence, Kansas became an important battleground over the issue of state's rights and the expansion of slavery. Also known as "Bleeding Kansas" and "Bloody Kansas," the Border Wars were a series of violent political confrontations between Kansan settlers from southern slave-owning states, and New England and Mid-Atlantic States.

10. In 1919, the sweetest disaster in history occurred—the Boston Molasses Disaster. A 2-million-gallon tank of molasses at the Purity Distilling Company collapsed, unleashing a 25-foot tall wave of surprisingly fast molasses into the streets, killing 21 and injuring 150.

11. Atlanta was once called Terminus, meaning "End of

the Line." In the plans to lay out the start and end points of the Western and Atlantic Railroads, the zero milepost was there, reading "Terminus."

12. Martin Van Buren, born in 1782, was the first US president to have actually been born in the United States of America as a newly independent nation. He was the 8th US president.

13. Abraham Lincoln, born in 1809, was a world class wrestler with only one recorded defeat (in 1832) under his belt in his twelve-year career with the sport. He was also reportedly an accomplished trash talker prior to developing his leadership skills.

14. On October 14, 1912, while campaigning for a second presidential term in Milwaukee, Theodore Roosevelt was shot in the chest by a saloon keeper. He went on moments later to deliver a ninety-minute speech, opening with the words, ""Friends, I shall ask you to be as quiet as possible. I don't know whether you fully understand that I have just been shot, but it takes more than that to kill a Bull Moose..."

15. In 1965, California Senator George Murphy joined the US Senate and was provided a desk near the busy entrance to the floor. He developed a habit of keeping the desk stocked with candy for himself and fellow

senators, even though eating is prohibited on the Senate floor. Republican senators have since maintained the tradition of the "candy desk," with each newly assigned recipient of the desk keeping the custom.

16. While preparing to give a speech to a Lions Club in Leary, Georgia, in 1969, Jimmy Carter and several witnesses noticed an unidentified flying object. Carter was asked to file an official UFO report in 1973 detailing the incident after being sworn in as governor of Georgia.

17. Over 150 years, the Anheuser-Busch Beer Company passed from father to son for five generations. A true family company, likened to "American royalty," custom had it that each firstborn of the new generation had a few drops of Budweiser beer placed onto his tongue before ever tasting his first drop of mother's milk.

18. The origin of the mid-inning break in baseball games is disputed, but one popular story of its beginning is attributed to President William Howard Taft, who, tall and overweight, was sore from sitting at an April 1910 game. He stood up to stretch, and the crowd felt obligated to follow the President's lead.

19. The Battle of Fort Carillon, fought at what is now Fort Ticonderoga on the NY side of Lake Champlain, was the bloodiest battle of the French and Indian War, marking over 3000 casualties, of which 2000 were British and 400 were French. The battle is cited as a textbook example of supreme military incompetence.

20. William Harding, often ranked as the worst and most incompetent of the first 31 US Presidents, was an avid gambler who once lost an entire White House china set dating back to the Presidency of Benjamin Harrison. He bet the entire set on a single hand— and lost.

# TEST YOURSELF

1. Why was the United States Civil War fought?

   A) Expansion into Mexico was opposed in the West.

   B) The North wanted to secede.

   C) The South was dependent on slavery.

2. Which president did not survive (or die from) an assassination attempt?

   A) Howard Taft

   B) Theodore Roosevelt

   C) Abraham Lincoln

3. Who is the only US President who has filed a UFO sighting report?

   A) Bill Clinton

   B) Jimmy Carter

   C) Gerald Ford

4. What was Jesse James known for?

   A) He killed Doc Holliday

   B) Lana Turner's daughter killed him

   C) He was the Robin Hood of Western outlaws

5. What was President Theodore Roosevelt known for?

A) Continuing a speech after an assassination attempt

B) Betting and losing the White House china

C) Keeping a candy drawer in the Resolute Desk

## ANSWERS

1. C
2. A
3. B
4. C
5. A

# CHAPTER SEVEN

# AMERICAN CULTURE

Part of the beauty of the United States of America is the complexity and intricacy of the tapestry woven by the intermingling of cultures to form one, with a few strong themes of old white European men, Native American heritage, and African-American traditions adapted from roots torn from their earth long ago. There are things to be ashamed of in the history, and things to be proud of— funny, sad, embarrassing, and frankly confusing things— but what makes the country truly fascinating is a richness of diversity found in no other on Earth. In this chapter are just a few of the strange, important, or just interesting tidbits of American culture.

## American Flag

The current United States flag was created by then seventeen-year-old Robert Heft in 1958. It was created for a class project on which he received a B-. Legend says that seamstress Betsy Ross sewed the first flag in 1776, after church member George Washington asked her to do so. This may not be true, as at least two others lay claim to the first flag's creation as well, but Betsy's story is the one that made history.

The original flag held thirteen red and white alternating stripes representing the thirteen colonies, with thirteen white stars on a blue field. On today's design, we still have the alternating stripes, but the fifty stars represent each of the fifty states. The design itself has changed twenty-six times. The colors are symbolic—red stands for valor, blue for vigilance, and white for purity. Some nicknames for the flag include "Stars and Stripes," "Old Glory," and "The Star-Spangled Banner."

## Statue of Liberty

The Statue of Liberty is a copper cultural icon residing in the harbor of New York City. It was given to the United States by the French in 1886. It's a UNESCO World Heritage Site and stands more than three hundred feet tall from its base. The robed woman is Libertas, a Roman goddess who represents freedom from tyranny, and the tablet she carries has the date July 4, 1776 engraved upon it. She has broken chains at her feet and a torch in her hand. The crown resembles a halo and calls to mind the sun gods.

A quote from an Emma Lazarus sonnet, New Colossus, is mounted inside the pedestal and says, "Give me your tired, your poor, your huddled masses yearning to be free." The significance to immigrants is noteworthy. Due to her location, she was the sign to new immigrants they had arrived in the United States.

## Groundhog Day

A strange cultural tradition no American can really explain, Groundhog Day is when we find out if winter will last six more weeks or if spring is on its way. Folklore says if the groundhog sees its shadow (meaning it's sunny out), he'll retreat to his den and winter will persist. The groundhog most of America watches is in Pennsylvania and is called Punxsutawney Phil. Groundhog Day began as a strange adaptation of weather lore in the eighteenth century so that the original belief is faintly recognizable now, but the first reference appears to be in 1841.

Groundhog Day enthusiasts claim the predictions are accurate up to 90 percent of the time, but actual science and data recording show the talentless hack of a groundhog only has 39 percent accuracy, and it's been getting worse in recent years.

## Kennedy Family

The Kennedy family is a political dynasty in the United States whom everyone knows, and depending on the person or topic, evokes emotions of awe or intimidation. Rumor says that patriarch Joe amassed the family's fortune through Prohibition bootlegging. Actually, he made his money on investments and was in the liquor import business, all boringly legal, and the bootlegger rumors started when son John started campaigning for presidency as an effort to discredit the candidate.

John, the second oldest of Joe's children and beloved American president, had eight siblings. While the family has been quite successful and is beloved by most of America, there is a fear and curiosity about them because of the "Kennedy curse." Of nine children, eldest Joseph Jr, was killed in World War I, and John and Robert (a popular senator) were assassinated in the 1960s. Rosemary had a lobotomy at age 23 that failed and left her incapacitated. Kathleen died young in a plane crash, and middle child Eunice, who founded the Special Olympics out of love for her sister Rosemary, ended up the oldest before her time. Patricia and Ted (a beloved but controversial long-serving United States senator) both lived full lives like Eunice, and youngest child Jean, who was once US ambassador to

Ireland, is the only child of the generation still living.

Joe's grandchildren have largely escaped the Kennedy Curse, but John, Jr. died in a plane crash with his wife, and Robert's widow has lost two of their eleven children to tragedy. Ted's oldest child died in middle age a couple of years after his death. The Kennedy family for a time was seen as our own American royalty, but they had secrets that kept us just as hooked as their charisma. The youngest generations have taken over the humanitarian roles their parents held but have chosen largely to stay out of the spotlight.

## Hot dogs — A taste of America

America's food palate is diverse and that's probably because it's a reflection of our immigrant culture. As we'll discuss more in a moment, there aren't too many American foods, and the ones we have are kind of accidents. No exception for the beloved and very American hot dog. In 1901, it was invented by Harry Stevens, a Brit if we're being completely honest, but we're not going to give up our claim to hot dogs as an American food over something so trivial. Stevens sold food concessions at baseball games, and at the New York Giants 1901 opener, he accidentally created the iconic food when he ran out of paper to serve the sausages. He put them on bread instead, and the rest is delicious history.

## Blackbeard

Edward Teach—or maybe you've heard of him as Blackbeard—was a fearsome pirate in the early eighteenth century. He had a long thick beard and lit fuses under his hat to scare people. His ship, the Queen Anne's Revenge, was a captured French ship that he equipped with a battalion of weaponry and lived aboard with his crew as he worked up and down the Southern east coast of the United States until settling down in Bath, North Carolina.

Blackbeard was the most fearsome pirate of his time. In his most well-known act of terror, he blockaded access to Charleston's ports for a week, seizing ships that entered or tried to leave, and holding some as prisoners for ransom. Choosing Bath to live in was his undoing, as the small town was near the Virginia border, and in 1718 he was killed by sailors with orders from the Virginia governor. The contingent from the Royal Navy returned to the governor with Blackbeard's severed head hanging from the boat's bow as evidence of their success.

## Smokey the Bear

Smokey the Bear is a cultural icon, a cartoon character the United States Forest Service uses to remind park goers to not start forest fires. But not many people know he was actually a real bear. In 1950, forest rangers were trying to contain a wildfire when they found the orphaned bear cub badly burned on the edge of the danger zone. They rescued him and rehabilitated him, with news spreading quickly. All news outlets picked up the story of the adorable bear cub who had been rescued from certain death after losing his family.

The Forest Service wisely used his newfound fame to start a conservation program that is still going strong today. He was well-cared for in a zoo until he died of old age in 1976. He received during his lifetime so many letters and gifts of honey that he was awarded his own ZIP code. He is buried at Smokey Bear Historical Park in Capitan, New Mexico, and his cartoon image can still be seen all over the United States, reminding children and adults alike that "Only YOU can prevent forest fires!"

## Weird Museums

From the big, bright lights of Las Vegas to the small knick-knacks that adorn our homes, Americans love kitsch. Leave it to a few industrious folks to turn their collections into money makers or to memorialize that which we all adore. The United States is a country full of history and museums, but some are light-hearted, and some cases, not so much but very, very weird. Check out a few of our strangest museums:

## Warren Anatomical Museum, Boston

This place is full of all kinds of strange things about the human body from fascinating to quirky to dark.

## Mutter Museum, Philadelphia

Similar to the Warren Museum but on a different level, this medical museum contains specimens, models, and antique equipment—and Einstein's brain. Like, the real brain, not a model.

## National Mustard Museum, Middleton WI

Do you like mustard? Not as much as Barry Levenson, who was questioning the meaning of life in the grocery store after being devastated the Boston Red Sox lost the 1986 World Series. The mustard spoke to him. I don't know what mysteries of life the mustard revealed, but that's the story, and so he opened a museum to honor the mustard. Really.

## Historic Auto Attractions, Roscoe IL

The exhibits in this place are mostly famous cars from TV or movies, such as the Batmobile and the Ghostbusters car. It features a lot of other things too though, like presidential memorabilia.

## Chasing Rainbows Museum, Pigeon Forge TN

This one is dedicated completely to country music superstar and American icon Dolly Parton, and I think that's all that needs to be said to sell you on that one.

## Musee Conti Wax Museum and the Pharmacy Museum, New Orleans

Both very different museums, they're lumped together because you've seen wax museums and you've seen pharmacies. But you've never seen either quite like this. With elaborate wax statues in detailed vignettes, you'll spend hours at the Musee Conti. The Pharmacy Museum is a fascinating peek into history. You used to feed WHAT to children?!?! They're both in New Orleans, so they can both be visited on your next trip.

## Toilet Seat Art Museum, Alamo Heights TX

The name pretty much says it all here. It is a sight to behold, and the owner takes his collection of hand-painted custom toilet seats very seriously.

## UFO Museum, Roswell NM.

Because of course there is a UFO museum in Roswell.

## Melting pot

The metaphor of a "melting pot" is often used to describe the United States. Because it is a nation of immigrants, it is a fusion of cultures and ethnicities, focusing on assimilation into the culture. Some recoil from this concept, as assimilation has heavy connotations in American history. However, it can be viewed as a metaphor to put many ingredients together and have them create a larger fine delicacy, and that's the imagery many thought they were evoking.

While the symbolism had been presented before, the term "melting pot" comes from a 1908 play of the same name, the opening night of which was even attended by President Theodore Roosevelt, who raved compliments about it. The main character emigrates to the United States after a Russian pogrom in which his entire family is killed. He creates a symphony which expresses his desire for all ethnicity to "melt away" so that everyone is treated the same. Then, of course, he falls in love, but not with just anyone! She's a Russian Christian, and her father is the officer responsible for murdering his family. He expresses his guilt, and everyone lives happily ever after.

Hopefully, with 20/20 hindsight, a play with that sort of message being used for the United States to praise assimilation and the concept of a "melting pot" can help people understand why perhaps diversity should be valued instead of sameness. Should we so easily forgive past sins of a nation? The messaging seems pointed, but it might be time for a different take. Perhaps better to disregard the melting pot and create a big stew, all separate and unique but wonderful together.

## Population

The United States of America is the third largest country in the world and has a population of 325 million people. A child is born every 8 seconds, and a person dies every 12. A new immigrant moves to the United States every 33 seconds. Ninety percent of residents speak some level of English, but over 300 languages are spoken. It's known for being a more diverse country, but more than three quarters of people are white, 18 percent are Latino or Hispanic, and more than 13 percent are black or African-American. Seventy-one percent of residents identify as Christians, but every known world religion is practiced to some extent. Twenty-three percent claim no religion, and 6 percent are non-Christian religious practitioners.

## Trashy folks

The Environmental Protection Agency says that we Americans throw away a whopping 4.4 pounds of trash every day—EACH. That's 1.4 billion pounds of trash daily, or 60,000 garbage trucks full. In a year, one person's trash is the same weight as a cow and the height of the Leaning Tower of Pisa. The whole country makes enough trash annually to reach to the moon and back 25 times. There's good news though—1.5 pounds of that daily trash are recycled or composted, and the US recycling rate is at an all-time high of about 35 percent. But does it make us less wasteful? Studies show that more recycling accompanies increased consumption behaviors and therefore more trash production as well. Perhaps the do-good feelings one has from recycling makes one feel comfortable purchasing a little more.

## We love food

It's a fairly common observation that the USA doesn't really have its own food culture. Perhaps because the culture is such a melting pot, most commonly consumed foods come from other countries, and food preferences vary wildly in different regions of the United States. Pizza is Italian, hamburgers come from Germany, and we love Chinese and Mexican food. Even the distinctive eats of the American South are mostly variations of African dishes, as food culture in the South grew from the skills of slaves who prepared the daily meals. Popular foods which are uniquely

American include things like chocolate chip cookies—but even cookies originated in Persia, we just added the chips—and popcorn. Now that one is actually American, no question. Native Americans were popping corn in 3600 BC.

## 'America'?

The United States of America is frequently referred to, both in the US and worldwide, as simply "America," and its' residents often "Americans." This is not appreciated by many Canadians and Latin Americans, for likely obvious reasons. They too are from the continents of either North or South America and are Americans as well. And depending on where one is from in the world, there are either seven or six continents, because some of us learn North America and South America as two separate continents, while others learn them as subcontinents of one large continent called The Americas. Making things more complicated, North America includes Central America and the Caribbean islands, and Central America is sometimes also considered a subcontinent, and Mexico is part of North America but culturally has more in common with its southern neighbors of Central America.

Fun bonus fact: Europe and Asia have the same debate. Maybe not over names and designations, but are they two continents or two subcontinents of Eurasia? So maybe there are five continents. No one knows; we're all confused.

## America's only true art form

The musical stylings of jazz get the title of America's only true art form. Although it's inspired by the rhythms and culture of Africa, combined in part with the classical music of western Europe, it was created here and become an art form that is all America's own. New Orleans is its birthplace, at least officially, and New Orleans does such a good job of keeping it alive and ever-evolving that we don't mind letting them have the title.

But truthfully, jazz developed in plantation fields all over the South. What makes jazz most unique is improvisation. Music is usually painstakingly written and practiced until it becomes routine, but jazz developed while hands and minds were busy with other tasks of survival. While slaves worked, they passed time and filled the air with music, and often they used it to send coded or not so coded messages—hence the improvisation that makes it unique. The improvisation helped their mood and focus, and gave the singers and audience ways to converse when they weren't otherwise permitted to. It was also a way to pass on and respond to stories – part of the rich African-American tradition of oral storytelling.

## Trick or treat, smell my feet

Trick or treating is a Halloween custom for children in many countries, but it takes on a life of its own in the United States. Children wear costumes and travel through their neighborhoods (or churches, or other organized locations, depending on the community) collecting candy. Traditionally, the children say to the candy bearer "Trick or treat!" and they receive candy in response. If someone refuses to give candy though, the threat is that the child will play some sort of prank on them. This is generally an idle threat, but November 1st is a morning Americans traditionally wake up to sugar highs and quick surveys of the neighborhood to see which neighbors need help removing toilet paper from trees and egg yolks from siding.

But its history, like the rest of most things American, is weirder than most of us know – it's actually a pretty ancient tradition in which Celts believed that the dressing as a demon was a defense mechanism to keep the real ones from messing with you. They celebrated the end of the year in costume to blend with the spirits, believing that as we pass from one year to another the dead and the living overlap. Because you could encounter a demon at any time in this transition period, you had to convince them you were on their side.

Fast forward to the years of the Catholic Church, and they were a little uncomfortable with everyone pretending to be evil during the celebrations, so costumes became more diverse – saints and angels mixed in with the demons, and now we have Elsas and Batmans too.

# INTERESTING FACTS

1. The United States does not have an official language, although English is used in government and is the most commonly spoken language among residents.

2. The national bird and the national animal of the United States is the bald eagle. It is found on the country's seal and was chosen because of its long life and strength, believed at the time in 1782 to only exist on this continent.

3. The population of the country is 327,000,000, which is about four percent of the world population and is the third most populous country in the world. In 1955, the population was roughly half that number, but it has always been number three.

4. Starbucks Coffee was founded in 1971, in Seattle, Washington. Today, it is one of the most widely-recognized household brands and is the face of coffee in the international markets, with 24,000 stores in 70 countries.

5. Montana has three times more cows than it does people and the largest grizzly bear population in the lower 48 states. With a million people, that means there are three

million cows. There are only 800 grizzlies though; the entire country hosts just 1,800.

6. The United States has a higher prison population than anywhere in the world. There are 2.3 million people in more than 5,000 correctional facilities, or 724 people for every 100,000 general population.

7. There are 100 acres of pizza sold every day. The most popular topping is pepperoni, and the much-maligned pineapple is number nine. Every region of the country has its preferences for pizza styles, and there are variations within.

8. America's deadliest job is that of President of the United States. Four of the forty-five presidents have been assassinated, which is a very high 9 percent.

9. One in every ten Americans is a descendent of at least one of the 102 original Mayflower pilgrims from 1620, but there may be more than 35 million direct descendants.

10. According to the World Giving Index, Americans are among the most likely people in the world to help a stranger. In 2013 and 2014, it was the highest ranked country, but was dethroned by Myanmar in 2015.

11. "The Highest Court in the Land" isn't the Supreme

Court of the United States. It's a basketball court. That is the nickname for the fifth-floor basketball court located in the Supreme Court building.

12. According to the National Football League, Super Bowl Sunday is the third largest occasion to consume food. It's right behind Christmas and Thanksgiving.

13. Fortune cookies aren't a Chinese food. They were invented in the United States in either the late 19th century or early 20th, and their origin is hotly contested. It became a war of sorts between San Francisco and Los Angeles, with a federal court intervening in San Francisco's favor. The city of Los Angeles officially condemned the decision.

14. Americans send an estimated 900 million Valentine's Day cards every year, making it the second largest day for card-giving in the country, behind Christmas.

15. There's a false story that Disney animators used Marilyn Monroe's body as the inspiration for Tinkerbell. Actually, the model was Margaret Kelly, who voiced a mermaid in *Peter Pan* and was at the time the titleholder for "Most Beautiful Legs in Hollywood." When she and her husband attended a screening of the film, he observed "Margaret, I'd recognize those thighs anywhere.

16. Presidents bowed to greet people until Thomas Jefferson started shaking hands. George Washington bowed in order to avoid physical contact, and it was continued until Jefferson, who wanted to be more personable.

17. The first reality show was MTV's "The Real World", a series about real people with real jobs, living their real lives. This ongoing series was actually inspired by an HBO reality special called An American Family, a documentary about a 1971 family going through divorce.

18. In 1996, US gymnast Kerri Strug broke her ankle on landing a vault during the Summer Olympics. She stuck the landing, earned a perfect 10, and helped the United States win gold.

19. President John F. Kennedy was the orator who famously said, "My fellow Americans, ask not what your country can do for you; ask what you can do for your country."

20. There are 27 Amendments to the US Constitution, but over 1100 have been proposed. Some of the most interesting failures: the effort to revoke US citizenship from anyone who accepts a title of nobility from a foreign nation, the criminalization of drunkenness, one to eliminate the presidency, and a movement to rename the USA United States of Earth.

# TEST YOURSELF

1. How did Joe Kennedy amass the Kennedy fortune?

   A) He was a businessman.

   B) He was a bootlegger during Prohibition.

   C) He was a famous writer.

2. Who designed the current flag?

   A) Betsy Ross

   B) George Washington

   C) A high school student

3. What is America's deadliest job?

   A) Disney animator

   B) President of the United States of America

   C) Prison guard

4. What is America's favorite pizza topping?

   A) Extra cheese

   B) Pepperoni

   C) Pineapple

5. Who is Libertas?

   A) President Andrew Jackson's wife

   B) The women who sewed the first flag

   C) The Statue of Liberty

**ANSWERS**

1. A
2. C
3. B
4. C
5. C

# CHAPTER EIGHT

# AMERICAN GEOGRAPHY

The terrain of the United States America ranges from beachy oceanside to rocky mountain, rivers to volcanoes, and all in between. Within its borders are some of the oldest mountains, some of the tallest, oldest, and longest rivers, volcanoes long dormant, and some that have reawakened in modern history with mighty bangs. The country has grown, and its landscape changed due to natural disaster and geopolitical forces. By land area, it's one of the largest countries and is geographically diverse. Without a doubt, the ground itself is as interesting as the social and political history.

## Denali—Highest mountain in the world or just the tallest?

The highest peak in North America proudly towers over the rest from Alaska, and the only higher mountains in the world are Mount Everest on the China/Nepal border and Aconcagua in Argentina. By one measure it is actually higher than Everest, even though official measurements have its elevation at only two-thirds Everest's. Measuring from base to summit, Everest is in fact two-thirds the size of Denali, but Everest has the highest elevation because its base is much higher.

Denali is, of course, the showcase of Denali National Park, which is so big the entire state of Massachusetts can fit inside. The Koyukon indigenous have called the peak "Denali", meaning "tall" for centuries, but it's been known to the United States government as Mount McKinley since its "discovery" in 1896 by a prospector who was a fan of not-yet-President William McKinley, who was in the midst of a successful campaign at the time. Alaska officially declared the mountain's name Denali in 1975, and the United States finally followed suit in 2015. The first successful ascent of the mountain wasn't until 1913, and since then, as the area has become more explored, the route has gotten easier with almost sixty percent succeeding. It takes two to four weeks to summit, and is one of the Seven Summits—the most challenging peaks from every continent, which the most serious of climbers attempt to conquer.

## Key West—The westernmost key on the east coast at the southernmost point of the USA

Key West is a kitschy little tourist town in the Florida Keys, adored by many for its rich history, unforgettable sunsets, colorful cast of characters, and constant party atmosphere. It's the southernmost point in the United States, only ninety miles from Cuba but almost double that to the closest Florida city of Miami. While the key is the furthest west of the Florida Keys, that's not actually how it got its name. It was called Cayo Hueso (Bone Cay) because it was a mass burial ground for indigenous people, but early explorers misunderstood the pronunciation and "Key West" stuck. The sunsets are celebrated every day with a festival on Duval Street, and the coral reef that extends from the key to the Dry Tortugas National Park is the third largest in the world behind The Great Barrier Reef off Australia and the Belize Barrier Reef.

The town's most beloved inhabitants aren't any of the locals that make it so unique or the tourists that rotate in and out—they're the town's chickens and the Hemingway cats. Yes, the town has free-roaming chickens, so precious to the residents that with the threat of major hurricane, the chickens are evacuated with the people. The Hemingway cats are arguably even more special. In the former residence of Ernest Hemingway, now a museum, around fifty cats, mostly polydactyl, reside quite happily. Tourists flock to the home to see them more so than to look into Hemingway's life.

They aren't evacuated during hurricane. Instead, volunteers and staff members at the museum risk their own lives and hunker in place to keep caring for the cats.

## Yellowstone

Yellowstone National Park is the oldest national park in the United States. In fact, the United States has the oldest national park system in the world, and Yellowstone was the first national park anywhere, established in 1872. (Some data disputes that, saying Mongolia has an older national park.) The park is so vast and complex that official measurements haven't been established, but it's approximately 3,472 square miles, larger than Rhode Island and Delaware combined, and is located mostly in Wyoming, with 3 percent crossing the border into Montana and 1 percent in Idaho. There is a wealth of interesting statistics to keep throwing into the knowledge bank about Yellowstone. There are almost thirty associated Native American tribes, with more than 1,800 archaeological sites and 25 sites on the National Register of Historic Places, and it contains part of the historic Nez Perce Trail, where the tribe of the same name attempted to flee the Army to avoid being forced onto a reservation.

It's also home to Old Faithful, a geothermal geyser that erupts from the ground every 45 minutes to two hours. It

170

shoots thousands of gallons of boiling water up to 185 feet into the air. The phenomenon was first observed in 1807 by a member of the Lewis and Clark expedition and then confirmed by another explorer nearly seventy years later, but both were rebuffed and called delusional. Yellowstone boasts almost 1,300 geysers, more than 75 percent of the known geysers in the world, and more than half of the world's geothermal features.

## Deadliest volcano in the United States

Mount Saint Helens was a dormant volcano until its 1980 eruption, which killed 57 people and was the most catastrophic volcanic event in United States history. It could have killed far more, but for two factors: warning signs led to evacuation, and it occurred on a Sunday when loggers weren't working the mountainside. In March, trouble began with a 4.2 earthquake, and by the end of April the entire north end of the volcano was bulging. This is a common prediction of eruption as magma builds below the surface, usually only detectable by specialized equipment, but in this case, it grew by five to six feet per day for about a month.

On May 18, after 10,000 earthquakes, a 5.1 caused a rockslide on the north face—the largest landslide ever recorded—and opened up the entire mountain, causing the volcano to blow from its side and changing the Oregon landscape permanently as the mountain took on a distinguishable crater. The eruption was 1,600 times the size of the Hiroshima atomic bomb.

There were five more eruptions through October of that year and at least 21 periods of eruption through 1990. Smaller eruptions have continued, with the volcano's activity increasing again to be concerning as recently as 2016. The United States Geological Survey says there is no sign it will erupt again soon but that it is very much alive.

## Mount Rushmore, checkmate

Most Americans know about Mount Rushmore near Keystone, South Dakota, where the images of Presidents George Washington, Thomas Jefferson, Theodore Roosevelt, and Abraham Lincoln are carved into the face of the mountain. But there's some interesting trivia most don't know. For instance, why those four? Well, it was the sculptor Gutzon Borglum who decided, and he simply felt they were the most important at the time. Washington was our first President and represents the birth of the nation. Jefferson wrote most of the Declaration of Independence and spearheaded the Louisiana Purchase—he represents growth. Roosevelt represents development because under his leadership the nation experienced rapid economic growth. Finally, Lincoln is the face of preservation because he held the country during Civil War.

But there's controversy surrounding the monument and a little sweet revenge. The land was originally Lakota and was seized after the Great Sioux War of 1876. In retaliation, less than twenty miles away, the Lakota commissioned a statue of Crazy Horse on horseback, nine times taller than the Rushmore sculptures. Crazy Horse was a Lakota warrior who fought federal encroachments. While the work began in 1948, it isn't scheduled to be completed for some time. It's worth mentioning, the site has government approval. The barren rock land was gifted to Henry Standing Bear in exchange for his fertile acres. Some Lakota also don't approve, citing violated Lakota customs and beliefs.

## The only royal palace

Iolani Palace is the only royal home on United States territory, the Honolulu home of the Hawaiian monarchy from 1845 to the kingdom's overthrow, then for military operations and government functions from 1959, when Hawaii was admitted to the Union. The state's first governor moved operations and began renovating the site, opening it as a museum in 1978.

The palace is a recreation of the site as royal residence, including global hunts and repurchases of items sold by the post-coup government, and painstaking exact replication of the unrecoverable items. It's the only building of its architectural style, called American Florentine, and it had electricity before the White House. The last queen was imprisoned there in 1895, and it's said to be very paranormally active.

## The only leprechaun colony east of Ireland

The Guinness Book of World Records first granted Portland, OR's Mill Ends Park with Smallest Park in the World status in 1971. It is a circle with a diameter of two feet, making it 452 square inches in full area. In 1948, the area was constructed for installation of a light pole. The pole never arrived, and weeds appeared instead. The site was in front of the Oregon Journal building in the median of a busy street, and the office planted flowers. They dedicated it on St. Patrick's Day of that year, naming it after a column in the paper, and claimed it to be a leprechaun colony.

The writer of the namesake column, Dick Fagan, created a legend around the park, featuring it in his columns, and popularity grew. The people of Portland frequently lovingly decorate the park and take care of it.

## How an earthquake sort of caused the Trail of Tears

In 1812, a series of earthquakes caused the soil beneath the Mississippi River to rise, causing it to flow backward. This is not that unusual an occurrence, having occurred recently after a hurricane, but this was the first time it appears to have been noticed or recorded—or at the very least, it was noticed and was very, very bad timing. A group of Muskogee Indians believed it to be Tie Snake, the river god, writhing underground. Some believed it was the god calling for the people to return to traditional ways and not allow Europeans to infiltrate the culture.

Around this time, the Spanish gave the Muskogee weapons, hoping they would war with the Americans. This led to the Muskogee War, which settlers instigated because they caught wind the Indians were debating an attack. Not-yet-president General Andrew Jackson led several attacks to defeat the Muskogees, a branch of Creek Indians. He didn't forget the experience, and when he became president, his policies led to the 1830 Indian Removal Act, from which came the Trail of Tears.

## The lowest high point and other oddities

Florida's highest point above sea level is Britton Hill, 345 feet in elevation. Naturally, it's about two miles from the Alabama state line. The next highest point outside that geographical region but still within Florida is Sugarloaf Mountain in Clermont, on Lake Apopka, which is actually the fifth highest point in the state and, as you may have guessed, not even remotely a mountain. It's a sand hill and has been stripped by logging, but was once a pine forest. Now it's mostly residential with a few citrus plantations and vineyards.

California has the lowest low point in the country, at 282 feet below sea level, Badwater Basin in Death Valley. The salt flats at Badwater are five miles long. It only fills at most with a thin sheet of standing water after significant rainstorm events that flood other parts of the valley.

## Alaska: Your Next Beach Vacation

The coastline of Alaska is longer than the rest of the US states' coastlines together. At 6,640 miles, second place Florida at 1,350, and California and Hawaii who combined come in at under 1,600 miles, pale in comparison. In fact, if you include islands, not just the mainland, Alaska covers just under 34,000 miles of shoreline.

There are also three million Alaskan lakes of significant size—over twenty acres—and it has more inland water than any other state, with more active glaciers than any other inhabited place in the world.

## Santa Claus, USA

There are three towns in the United States called Santa Claus, and one in Idaho that got sloppy and just went with Santa. They're just a handful of the Christmas-obsessed locales in the country, from cities who annually try to outdo one another with over-the-top celebrations, to cities who are built on celebrating the holiday year-round.

Santa Claus, Indiana, is the largest of the three, with a population slightly over 2,000. Located on the Ohio River, most people live in a development called Christmas Lake Village, with three lakes—Christmas Lake, Lake Holly, and Lake Noel. This town is full of Christmas cheer.

Santa Claus, Georgia, has a population of 250, and they go all out, too. Most people live on streets with names like Rudolph's Way and Candy Cane Road. At Santa Claus City Hall, they keep the Christmas cheer and decor up year-round.

You may have never heard of Santa Claus, Arizona. That's because it's a ghost town— no residents anymore—and the last business closed in 1995. If you want to check it out, there's a wishing well, a derailed children's train, and plenty of abandoned buildings. These little elves went back to the North Pole. As of 2005, any mail addressed to Santa Claus, AZ, is sent to Indiana.

## "I can see Russia from my house!"

The United States (or Alaska, specifically) and Russia are separated by a thin waterway called the Bering Strait. It's 53 miles across at its narrowest point. Mainland Asia and North America are a little hard to see from one another, but there are two small islands in the center of the Strait. Little Diomede of the United States and Big Diomede of Russia are only 2.5 miles away from one another. Little Diomede is inhabited by just over one hundred people, the native Inupiat Eskimo.

Mail on Little Diomede is the only contract in the nation that has to be delivered by helicopter—it's that isolated. There is no running water, houses are built on stilts, and the airport runway must be carved out of ice. Before the Cold War, families lived on both Big Diomede and Little Diomede, crossing back and forth. In 1948, the border was closed, and separated relatives lamented the Ice Curtain. The residents of Big Diomede were forcibly moved to Siberia, on the mainland. The Russian island no longer has a permanent population.

## Appalachian Mountains — hard to pronounce, harder to spell, impossible to keep in one place

The Appalachian Mountains of the eastern United States are one of the oldest mountain ranges in the world, at about 680 million years, and at one time were higher than the Himalayas, but they're sinking below and eroding from the top. The range predates the creation of North America, having formed when plates collided to create the supercontinent of Pangaea, with the mountain range at about center. The Appalachians are the same mountain range that forms the Atlas Mountains of Morocco and Algeria, but when Pangaea split they bid farewell and promised to write often.

One of many wonders of the Appalachian Mountains is the manmade Appalachian Trail, a 2,170-mile hike from Maine to Georgia covering 14 states. Four thousand volunteers put in 175,000 hours every year to maintain the longest footpath in the world. Most hikers of the trail will never summit Everest, but if you hike the entire trail, it's the equivalent of climbing Everest sixteen times—a little warmer though.

## Sitting in traffic is the American way

For most cities, the population doesn't change a great deal from day to day or hour to hour, obvious exceptions to be made for small college towns. Manhattan is another story though. A weekday night, meaning mostly residents, sees about two million people (actual population, 1.6 million). During the weekday, this doubles to four million, and on a weekend the city hosts three million. Only eight percent of Manhattan commutes to other boroughs or cities to work every day.

Three New York City boroughs have the highest daytime decrease in population in the nation, meaning residents of Queens, Brooklyn, and the Bronx greatly contribute to Manhattan's increase. It depends largely on job sector how long a person's average commute is, but the finance sector has the highest average at just under an hour. However, there are many commuters who travel up to two hours from surrounding states.

## Swampland is prime real estate

The city of Houston, Texas, has always been known for severe flooding, growing worse with climate change, and at its most deadly in 2017 after Hurricane Harvey. The largest city in Texas and fourth largest in the United States, the city of 2.3 million is almost two hundred years old.

But why does it flood so badly? The answer is surprisingly simple, and possibly concerning. It was built on a swamp. The city is only fifteen meters above sea level and is very flat. The highest area is only about forty feet higher than the average. Prior to development, it was marshland and swampland, with a bit of forest and prairie for good measure.

To an average person, building a city on a swamp sounds like an astonishingly bad idea. It isn't uncommon though. Chicago and New Orleans (which is also prone to serious flooding) were built on swamps. Part of Washington, D.C., was too. It's not just an American concept either—so were London, Berlin, and Moscow.

# INTERESTING FACTS

1.  Rhode Island is the smallest state in the United States of America at just 1,545 square miles, and Alaska is the largest. It is 663,268 square miles.

2.  The most crooked street in the world is Wall Street. — DRUMROLL! — Just kidding, it's actually the aptly named Snake Alley in Burlington, Iowa, and if you get carsick, you probably shouldn't go.

3.  The President of the United States lives at 1600 Pennsylvania Avenue, also known as the White House. President John Adams was the first to live there in 1800. No one lived there from 1814-1817 during reconstruction after the British set fire to it in 1814. President George Washington selected the site in 1791.

4.  The Missouri River, 2,565 miles from start to finish, is the longest river in the United States. It starts in the Rocky Mountains of western Montana and enters the Mississippi River north of St. Louis, Missouri. When combined with the lower Mississippi, it is the world's fourth longest river system.

5.  There is enough water in Lake Superior to cover all of North America and South America in a foot of water.

That's 3 quadrillion gallons, incidentally.

6. The geographical center of the United States is in the state of Kansas, on a farm near Lebanon and about 12 miles from the Nebraska border.

7. The only diamond mine in the United States is in Murfreesboro, Arkansas. It's operated by the state as a pay-to-dig site for tourists, and up to a few hundred carats are found each year.

8. The world's most active volcano is Kilauea on the island of Hawaii. It's the youngest volcano on Hawaii, but it's been erupting constantly since 1983 and expands the island as lava cools in the sea and hardens into rock.

9. Did you know that Detroit, Michigan, is north of Canada? Well, part of it anyway. The city of Windsor is due south to Detroit because of a curve in the Detroit River.

10. There is a house in Rockport, Massachusetts, built entirely of newspaper. It was a summer home built in 1922, and became the hobby of mechanical engineer Elis Stenman, also known for designing the machine that makes paper clips.

11. The largest cactus plantation in the world is located in

Edwards, Mississippi. Did you know there are cactus plantations? Well, they actually claim it's the only one out there, but we found one in India. The Mississippi plantation is closed now but was recently purchased and is scheduled to reopen in Spring 2018.

12. Alaska is the westernmost and northernmost state in the USA, but it's also the easternmost. How is this possible? Parts go so far west that it stretches into the eastern hemisphere.

13. Every person in the world could fit into Texas if it were as densely populated as New York City. If it were populated like Houston, Texas would need to be seven times bigger.

14. There are eleven states with land further south than the northernmost point of the Mexican border. They are California, Texas, South Carolina, Hawaii, Georgia, Alabama, New Mexico, Arizona, Mississippi, Louisiana, and Florida.

15. From Stamford, CT, no matter what direction you travel, the next state over is New York. It's thirty miles from Manhattan and part of the New York City metro area.

16. There are 43 buildings in Manhattan that have their

own ZIP code. These include the Empire State Building, The Chrysler Building, and two of the buildings in Penn Plaza.

17. Alaskans love a brisk commute. They walk to work every day more than in any other state in the country.

18. Battle Creek, Michigan, manufactures more breakfast cereal than any other city in the world. It's known as The Cereal Bowl.

19. Venus flytraps are native to a sixty square mile area of coastal bogs around the city of Wilmington, North Carolina, and absolutely nowhere else in the world.

20. A half-million earthquakes are felt in California annually.

# TEST YOURSELF

1. Name an American city not built on a swamp:

   A) Chicago

   B) Houston

   C) San Francisco

2. What city more than doubles in size every day?

   A) Miami

   B) Detroit

   C) New York City

3. What is one thing Alaska isn't known for?

   A) Most coastline in the country

   B) Most people who jog to work every day

   C) The easternmost point in the United States

4. You could climb Mount Everest, or you could hike the Appalachian Trial _____ times.

   A) 9

   B) 16

   C) 18

5. Where are Venus flytraps native to?

   A) New York City

B) Battle Creek, Michigan

C) Wilmington, North Carolina

# ANSWERS

1. A
2. C
3. B
4. B
5. C

# DON'T FORGET YOUR
# FREE BOOKS

# MORE BOOKS BY BILL O'NEILL

I hope you enjoyed this book and learned something new.

Please feel free to check out

some of my previous books on **Amazon**.

Made in the USA
San Bernardino, CA
14 May 2020

71771867R00111